Christopher Kendall
Wayne Martino
Editors

Gendered Outcasts
and Sexual Outlaws
Sexual Oppression
and Gender Hierarchies
in Queer Men's Lives

Pre-publication
REVIEWS,
COMMENTARIES,
EVALUATIONS . . .

"*Gendered Outcasts and Sexual Outlaws* explores issues about masculinity, effeminacy, and oppression within gay men's communities, mainly in the United States and Australia. Writing in a variety of genres, the authors show how mainstream cultural ideas about manhood and its privileges have power even within gay communities, with damaging consequences for many men as well as for women. This book proposes an original, indeed unique, combination of poststructuralist queer theory and antipornography feminism.

Its publication calls attention to the experience of men marginalized by the stigma of effeminacy. The highlights are a beautifully clear and compassionate account of what being raped means to men by Rus Ervin Funk, and a vivid and horrifying account of an abusive relationship in a short story by Peter Shuttlewood."

R. W. Connell, PhD
Professor of Education,
University of Sydney

CSUSM LGBTQA Pride Center

More pre-publication
REVIEWS, COMMENTARIES, EVALUATIONS . . .

"This is cutting-edge discussion and critical analysis, sorely needed in a world where masculinity has been defined within a framework of violence and control that moves between private and public spheres, where straight-acting gay men batter and rape male companions in private while condoning mistreatment of other gay men, women, and racial minorities in public. This collection lays a foundation that will enable further gay analysis of manhood and its consequences for gay men and for society as a whole. I welcome in this collection the voices that assist gay theory to shift outside the cultural framework of U.S. gay-think toward a more international critique of gay identities and practice, gender hierarchies, and sexual oppression. I recommend this work as a must-read."

Alison J. Laurie, PhD
Academic Programme Director,
Gender and Women's Studies,
Victoria University of Wellington,
New Zealand

"Kendall and Martino have compiled a powerful and pioneering collection of personal experiences and theoretical essays that don't shirk away from debates about masculinist hierarchies, misogyny, and racism within the gay community. While not undermining the work against heteronormativity and homophobia that is still required with the 'dominant outside,' this book calls for an honest and up-front engagement with the 'dominant inside': how straight-acting hypermasculinity, sissyphobia, consumerism, domestic violence, and pornography within the gay community may be complicit with and exploited by wider patriarchal heterosexist socioeconomic and political frameworks."

Maria Pallotta-Chiarolli, PhD
Senior Lecturer,
School of Health
and Social Development,
Deakin University,
Melbourne, Australia

HPP
Harrington Park Press®
An Imprint of The Haworth Press, Inc.
New York • London • Oxford

Gendered Outcasts and Sexual Outlaws

Sexual Oppression and Gender Hierarchies in Queer Men's Lives

HARRINGTON PARK PRESS®
Gay and Lesbian Studies
John P. De Cecco, PhD
Editor in Chief

From Drags to Riches: The Untold Story of Charles Pierce by John Wallraff

Lytton Strachey and the Search for Modern Sexual Identity: The Last Eminent Victorian by Julie Anne Taddeo

Before Stonewall: Activists for Gay and Lesbian Rights in Historical Context edited by Vern L. Bullough

Sons Talk About Their Gay Fathers: Life Curves by Andrew R. Gottlieb

Restoried Selves: Autobiographies of Queer Asian/Pacific American Activists edited by Kevin K. Kumashiro

Queer Crips: Disabled Gay Men and Their Stories by Bob Guter and John R. Killacky

Dirty Young Men and Other Gay Stories by Joseph Itiel

Queering Creole Spiritual Traditions: Lesbian, Gay, Bisexual, and Transgender Participation in African-Inspired Traditions in the Americas by Randy P. Conner with David Hatfield Sparks

How It Feels to Have a Gay or Lesbian Parent: A Book by Kids for Kids of All Ages by Judith E. Snow

Getting It On Online: Cyberspace, Gay Male Sexuality, and Embodied Identity by John Edward Campbell

Pederasts and Others: Urban Culture and Sexual Identity in Nineteenth-Century Paris by William A. Peniston

Men, Homosexuality, and the Gods: An Exploration into the Religious Significance of Male Homosexuality in World Perspective by Ronald E. Long

Mucho Macho: Seduction, Desire, and the Homoerotic Lives of Latin Men by Chris Girman

Side by Side: On Having a Gay or Lesbian Sibling edited by Andrew R. Gottlieb

Gay Catholic Priests and Clerical Sexual Misconduct: Breaking the Silence edited by Donald L. Boisvert and Robert E. Goss

Straight Talk About Gays in the Workplace: Creating an Inclusive, Productive Environment for Everyone in Your Organization, Third Edition by Liz Winfeld

Gendered Outcasts and Sexual Outlaws: Sexual Oppression and Gender Hierarchies in Queer Men's Lives edited by Christopher Kendall and Wayne Martino

The Cure for Sodomy by Ken Shakin

Gendered Outcasts and Sexual Outlaws

Sexual Oppression and Gender Hierarchies in Queer Men's Lives

Christopher Kendall
Wayne Martino
Editors

HPP

Harrington Park Press®
An Imprint of The Haworth Press, Inc.
New York • London • Oxford

For more information on this book or to order, visit
http://www.haworthpress.com/store/product.asp?sku=5437

or call 1-800-HAWORTH (800-429-6784) in the United States and Canada
or (607) 722-5857 outside the United States and Canada

or contact orders@HaworthPress.com

Published by

Harrington Park Press®, an imprint of The Haworth Press, Inc., 10 Alice Street, Binghamton, NY 13904-1580.

PUBLISHER'S NOTE
The development, preparation, and publication of this work has been undertaken with great care. However, the Publisher, employees, editors, and agents of The Haworth Press are not responsible for any errors contained herein or for consequences that may ensue from use of materials or information contained in this work. The Haworth Press is committed to the dissemination of ideas and information according to the highest standards of intellectual freedom and the free exchange of ideas. Statements made and opinions expressed in this publication do not necessarily reflect the views of the Publisher, Directors, management, or staff of The Haworth Press, Inc., or an endorsement by them.

Cover design by Kerry E. Mack.

Library of Congress Cataloging-in-Publication Data

Gendered outcasts and sexual outlaws : sexual oppression and gender hierarchies in queer men's lives / Christopher Kendall, Wayne Martino, editors.
     p. cm.
  Includes bibliographical references and index.
  ISBN-13: 978-1-56023-500-2 (hc. : alk. paper)
  ISBN-10: 1-56023-500-4 (hc. : alk. paper)
  ISBN-13: 978-1-56023-501-9 (pbk. : alk. paper)
  ISBN-10: 1-56023-501-2 (pbk. : alk. paper)
  1. Gay men—Social conditions. 2. Gay men—Identity. 3. Gender identity. 4. Masculinity. 5. Sexism. I. Kendall, Christopher N. II. Martino, Wayne.

HQ76.G36 2005
306.76'62—dc22

2005009948

To my partner, Jeremy Curthoys, for helping me say
the words that needed to be said.

—Chris

To my partner, Jose Medeiros, for his love and support.

—Wayne

CONTENTS

ABOUT THE EDITORS

Christopher Kendall, SJD, is a law professor and the former Dean of Law at Murdoch University in Perth, Western Australia. Originally from Winnipeg, Canada, Chris remains active in antipornography legal activism in Canada. In 2000, he was part of the legal team for 'Equality Now' before the Supreme Court of Canada in the case of Little Sisters Book and Art Emporium's case in which the Court agreed with Equality Now that same-sex pornography, like heterosexual pornography, violates the sex equality provisions of Canada's Charter of Rights and Freedoms. Chris has published extensively throughout Canada, Australia, and the United States on the pornographic abuse, misogyny, and racism within the gay male community.

Wayne Martino, PhD, is a Senior Lecturer in Education at Murdoch University in Perth, Western Australia. His research has explored the impact of masculinities and sexualities on boys'/men's lives at school. Dr. Martino is the co-author of *Boys' Stuff: Boys Talk About What Really Matters, What About the Boys: Issues of Masculinity in Schools,* and *"So What's A Boy?" Addressing Issues of Masculinity & Schooling.*

CONTRIBUTORS

Tim Bergling is a television news producer and journalist in Washington, DC, and the author of *Sissyphobia: Gay Men and Effeminate Behavior* (2001, Harrington Park Press) and *Reeling in the Years: Gay Men's Perspectives on Age and Ageism* (2003, Harrington Park Press). His work has appeared in *Genre, Out, Instinct, HERO,* and *Joey* magazines. A DC-area native, Bergling is a former U.S. Marine (1982-1990) who was among the contributors to the 2000 military short-story anthology *A Night in the Barracks* (Harrington Park Press). He is currently working on two more books—*Chasing Adonis: Gay Men and the Pursuit of Perfection* and *What Planet Are YOU From? Gay Men, Lesbians, and the Space Between.* One day he will complete his first full-length novel, as well as a collection of short stories. Check out his Web site at www.timbergling.com.

Rus Ervin Funk has been working as an activist and community organizer to address sexual and domestic violence since 1983. In addition to his therapeutic work with male victim-survivors, he has also provided intervention services with male perpetrators of domestic violence as well as with adolescent and adult sex offenders. Rus has also done work in public policy, including being one of the authors of the 1994 U.S. Violence Against Women Act. He is the founder of Men for Gender Justice, and the cofounder of DC Men Against Rape, the People's Coalition for Justice, the Washington Area Clinic Defense Task Force, and the Baltimore Alliance Against Child Sexual Abuse. In 2003, he cofounded MEN (Mobilizing to End Violence) and founded the Louisville Teen Dating Violence Network and the online discussion group Feminists Against Pornography and Prostitution. Rus is currently educator and trainer at the Center for Women and Families in Louisville, Kentucky. He also sits on the board of directors of the National Center on Domestic and Sexual Violence.

John Gascoigne is a twenty-two-year-old itinerant writer. He records his daily grind at www.charlton.diary-x.com.

Daryl Higgins is currently a senior research fellow at the Australian Institute of Family Studies. At the time of writing, he was a Senior Lecturer in the School of Psychology at Deakin University. Since 1998, he has been researching, publishing, and supervising students on a wide range of topics, including the nature of gay attraction, homophobia in schools, workplace stress and harassment, adolescent psychosocial problems, child abuse and family violence, and the child protection system.

Robert Jensen, PhD, is an associate professor in the School of Journalism at the University of Texas at Austin, where he teaches courses in media ethics, law, and politics. He is the coauthor of *Pornography: The Production and Consumption of Inequality,* and author of *Writing Dissent: Taking Radical Ideas from the Margins to the Mainstream* and *Citizens of the Empire: The Struggle to Claim Our Humanity.*

Anthony Lambert teaches media and cultural studies at Macquarie University. His PhD on the relationship between gender and land in Australian film and culture was awarded at the beginning of 2003. He is currently researching constructions of anticolonial identities as well as posthumanism and new gaming technologies.

Simon Obendorf, BA (Hons), LLB (Hons) (Melb.), is a doctoral candidate in the University of Melbourne's Department of Political Science. He serves on the Council of the Institute of Postcolonial Studies in Melbourne. Simon's current work explores the intersection of sexuality studies, postcolonialism, and studies of the international.

Peter Shuttlewood lives in Sydney with his partner of seven years. He is an accountant working in finance, administration, and information technology areas. His writing is infused with pop culture and pathos, blank prose and fierce fonts. He won first prize in the *OutRage* Short Story Competition in 1997 for "The Other Man"—a look at a gay ménage à trois.

Foreword

I wish I had read this book at some other time. Not now, while a reckless and fraud-based war is being waged because a certain son fears being viewed as a wimp. Not now, while clueless goons for his military are breaking down male prisoners for interrogation by shaming and humiliating them through pornographized same-sex sex acts. Not now, while this global superpower fueled by craven lust for masculine superiority is embarked on a suicidal folly that only further inflames the rage of insurgents and terrorists who *also* lust for masculine superiority—and who are determined not to stop till *their* manhood crushes the superpower's.

Or maybe now was exactly the right time to read this book—which is, after all, about the cultural misogyny that manifests as femiphobia, driving dominant definitions of manhood and ineluctably cascading from the pinnacles of hypermasculinity to the bottommost sissyness.

Gender is not a many-splendored thing. It makes the world go wrong. It means never having to say you're equal.

The radical feminist critique of gender—also known as male supremacy—has been around for quite a while now. The central finding of that critique—that gender is fundamentally a social caste system based on eroticized dominance and subordination—has been the topic of lively debate in the fields of law, philosophy, politics, theology, and other marketplaces of ideas. Activists have taken to heart this critique's implications for a groundbreaking new notion of justice, one that does not condone degradation or humiliation just because it induced an orgasm for someone somewhere. And a profound inquiry into human nature has been begun, seeking to understand whether the evolution of our species has resulted in an eroticism actually more desirous of mutual pleasure in communion than it is apparently hardwired for gratification in power-over.

Gender as a problematic has recently taken hold, in somewhat rarefied form, in the academy, where various "studiesists"—women's, men's, gender, queer—both assimilate the feminist analysis and attempt to dissociate from it at the same time. The theoretical gobbledygook that comes of their dance of approach/avoidance can be recognized, most prominently, as postmodernism: yes, gender is a troublesome construct, but we dare not undo it because we cannot imagine feeling sexy without it. Even as the tyranny of gender has increasingly suffused the body politic, embedding itself in both eroticism and economics, allegiance to the commerce of the sex industry (particularly pornography and prostitution) has largely bought off these academics' moral intelligences and dead-ended their investigations.

In everyday life, however, the tyranny of gender continues to rankle, intruding on individual consciousness episodically not as a specious aphrodisiac to which one must remain addicted but rather a wounding sex-class system in which one is imprisoned. And every day, real flesh-and-blood people bear witness to the longing to escape and heal.

The brave voices of a few of these folks can be heard on these pages. Each knows intimately some dimension of gender's devastating dynamics. Each is painfully familiar with some penalty that must be paid for gender nonconformity. And in some sense each struggles toward a model of human identity that does not depend on dominance, disidentification, and disdain.

What is most remarkable about these voices is that taken together they reveal gender as a caste system that depends not only on dominance of male over and against female but also on dominance of male over and against male. This political system purportedly based on natural sex difference in fact cannot exist without downward derogation, discrimination, and derision.

When you hear what these voices have to say, listen with some measure of gratitude. For they are helping to make the reality of the tyranny of gender palpable and visible—and thereby loosen its bonds on all our lives.

John Stoltenberg
Washington, DC
June 13, 2004

Part I:
The Dynamics of Sex/Gender Oppression

Part I of this book provides the work of seven men who challenge the assumptions that form the basis of queer male identity. Relying to a large extent on the work of radical feminism and cultural theorists, the authors explore what gender means to them within the context of a society in which men are expected to act according to norms governing the constitution of idealized forms of masculinity and in which they are penalized socially to the extent that they do not.

This section starts with an Introduction by Christopher Kendall and Wayne Martino. The authors outline what gender means in a society in which to be male equates with a certain form of power, while being female often equates with submission and sexual inferiority. Applying this social dynamic to the lives of queer men, the authors call for a radical rethinking of what it means to be male and, more specifically, a queer male. Designed to give space to those who are, within the queer community, positioned as "gendered outcasts" for the failure to conform, this chapter sets the tone for the work that follows: work from men who have refused to conform or who have paid the price for doing so.

Chapter 2 is a poem by John Gascoigne which articulates a desire for and validation of the culturally constructed notion of the feminine as opposed to its repudiation that is at the heart of the assimilation and appropriation of hegemonic masculinities in many gay men's lives. This blurring of gender boundaries and the gendered body signifies transgression and subversion. It interrupts the regulatory norms that govern the articulation of desire for many gay men, which is a theme that is taken up in this section of the book.

In Chapter 3, Robert Jensen takes up this idea of regulation through the imposition of identity categories and labels that limit and frame his own sexuality within a supposed "queer" community where he feels homeless. He writes about how the source of his struggle and alienation relates to the dissonance that is created from within the "queer" male community as a result of his conception of sexuality and radical feminist politics. He repudiates the familiar gendered and sexualized hierarchies that frame and regulate the articulation of desire as dictated by the "regulatory apparatus" of patriarchy to embrace the expression of one's sexuality as "an arena in which people have maximal freedom to explore themselves and others in relatively egalitarian relationships." It is in this sense that he questions the investment of gay male culture in sexual objectification and commodification and, hence, in systems of domination and untenable power relationships.

In Chapter 4, Tim Bergling also reflects on gender oppression, which takes the form of a rejection of effeminacy that functions as a policing mechanism in many gay men's lives. This piece serves as a postscript to his book *Sissyphobia* (Harrington Park Press), which was significant in highlighting these issues. In foregrounding the hatred and fear that many gay men have for "a man who behaves in an effeminate way," the *gendered outcast* takes center stage in his work. The responses to *Sissyphobia* that Bergling continues to receive and which are documented here attest to the significant impact that his work has had on the lives of many gay men.

In Chapter 5, Wayne Martino addresses this issue further in his discussion of the "repudiation of the feminine" in gay men's lives through an examination of the prevalence of the symbolic significance of "straight-acting masculinity" and its materialization in gay men's lives. He draws significantly on the work of Judith Butler and other writers such as Leo Bersani, Mark Simpson, Michelangelo Signorile, and Michael Alvear. He argues that bodies matter in terms of how corporeal masculinities get configured through a disavowal of the feminized Other in gay men's lives, which takes the form of the "feminized fag." The point that he makes is that "straight acting" signifies the full force of this compulsion and lived reality of embracing hegemonic masculinity for a significant number of gay men. He advocates a politics and ethics of male sexual practice and relatedness that rejects gender hierarchies, sexual oppression, and the idealization of certain power relationships in gay men's lives under the banner of sexual liberation.

In Chapter 6, Anthony Lambert explores further the issue of the idea of the "straight" masculine in his analysis of a range of physical and virtual spaces as sites where gay men constitute themselves as particular kinds of gendered and sexualized subjects. He argues that performing the "idealized masculine" is a means by which many gay men gain entry into a culture that validates certain ideals and stats such as a huge dick and a gym-toned and muscled body. He illuminates insightfully "how normalizing practices produce gay men, physically and psychically, as gendered outcasts, homosexual males whose environmental assimilation is made possible only through the enactment of a vocabulary that reduces both the visibility and value of difference."

In Chapter 7, Daryl Higgins also takes up issues regarding the gay male body but adopts a psychoanalytic focus on narcissistic masculinity and the Adonis complex. He explores the notion of how masculinity is constructed and the impact this has on the embodiment of gender in gay men's lives. Ultimately, he moves to addressing the relationship between masculinity, body absorption, and the notion of community. He reports on research that reveals that many gay men search for a partner who is similar to what "they would ideally like to be themselves." He traces in such desires the narcissistic tendency that is built on an idealization of masculinity and the Adonis complex.

Chapter 1

Introduction

Christopher Kendall
Wayne Martino

> Employing the subversive power of the unnatural to unseat the Platonic world view, the queer, unlike the rather polite categories of gay and lesbian, revels in the discourse of the loathsome, the outcast, the idiomatically-proscribed position of same-sex desire. Unlike petitions for civil rights, queer revels constitute a kind of activism that attacks the dominant notion of the natural. The queer is the taboo-breaker, the monstrous, the uncanny. Like the phantom of the Opera, the queer dwells underground, below the operatic overtones of the dominant; frightening to look at, desiring, as it plays its own organ, producing its own music. (Case, 1993:3)*

At the heart of sexual oppression and hierarchical power relations in queer men's lives lurks the "operatic overtones of the dominant" in the form of the gendered outcast. This often materializes, within the context of social and hierarchical relations among gay men, around a norm of bodily formation that produces "a domain of abjected bodies, a field of deformation" (Butler, 1993:16) that constitutes the not fully masculine. What often gets constituted within the limits of regulatory schemas for inscribing the normative means by which gay male subjects are formed in queer communities is a despised and repudiated Other. In fact, the feminized "fag" gets appropriated equally from within the gay male community with such a force that it raises ques-

---

*We would like to thank Dr. Anthony Lambert in the Department of Cultural Studies at Macquarie University for drawing our attention to this reference.

tions about just how taboo-breaking "queer" actually is for many gay men who subscribe to straight-acting and aestheticized masculinities (Simpson, 2003b, 2004) as well as forms of sexual oppression that get read as sexual liberation. In this chapter we raise some important issues about masculinities and sexual oppression in queer men's lives that are taken up further by contributors in this collection of essays. Our main argument is that the gendered outcast emerges from within the queer community to signify the full force of enforced normalization and idealization of masculinity in gay men's lives. Moreover, we argue that to constitute gay male pornography as a site for transformative possibilities for queer men (Dowsett, 1996; Warner, 1999) is to ignore equally its complicity in sexual oppression as well its anxiety-producing and normalizing potential. This is manifested in its reiterative capacity as a technology for installing norms around which the desirable and idealized gay male body gets articulated and represented. This is often instantiated within the context of the legitimation of certain eroticized power relations that are dictated from within the apparatus of heterosexuality. In other words, rather than "enabling disruption" or the "occasion for a radical rearticulation of the symbolic horizon in which bodies come to matter," what gets re-inscribed are familiar sexist and racialized power relationships in which the active/passive gender binary is inscribed.

SUBVERTING "THE UNNATURAL" OR REINSCRIBING THE DOMINANT GENDER ORDER?

What Signorile (1997) terms the "cult of masculinity" and how it gets played out in many gay men's lives in quite distinctive ways highlights the extent to which normalizing sex/gender regimes constitute regulatory and policing systems of self-surveillance and monitoring that produce a certain degree and intensification of anxiety around the body. But it is important to note, as emphasized by Simpson (2003b, 2004), that such an aestheticized, narcissistic, and self-conscious kind of masculinity, for which the gay male has been the prototype, has now been commercialized in the form of the metrosexual as a product of global market consumerism, spawned by the "frankenstein media monster." In what Simpson terms "a hyper-consumerist, post-industrial age of consumerism" which has impacted on all men, however, body fascism and anxieties about the embodiment of masculinity in gay men's lives continue to intensify. This is a result, according to Signorile, of the "identification with as well as desire for the sexual object" which leads to "many if not most of us becom[ing] both the rigidly objectified as well as the rigid objectifier, holding ourselves and each other to rigid standards" dictated by norms for eroticizing the male body (1997:16). This becomes evident in gay chat rooms where gym-toned bodies, a big dick, and straight-acting emerge as identificatory categories for establishing the basis of sexual desire for many gay men surfing the net for sex. Statements by gay men shopping for sex take the form of "No fems, no fats, no Asians!" or "Straight-acting only" followed by an apology or a rationalization that no offense is intended, it's just that they are not attracted to Asian or effeminate men. In fact, one gay man on gay.com was adamant that he "hated guys that carry on like girls . . . masculine gays only . . . if I wanted a woman I guess I would not be like a guy that is a man in every way."

As Butler highlights, (1993:187), this practice of reinforcing certain gender norms serves as a basis for compelling such eroticized identificatory practices of embodied masculinity (see Chapter 5). The imperative to embrace such norms often leads to inciting a deep-seated anxiety. This sense of the "traumatic" materializes for many gay men in their fears of effeminacy that lie at the basis of what signifies being a gay male. What seems to be driving this "cult of masculinity" enacted through body fascism is a rejection of what at the beginning of the twentieth century was the constitution of the gay men as gender inverts, as men trapped in women's bodies (see Signorile, 1997; Levine, 2004). In fact, historically it was through the apparatus of psychology that this knowledge about gay men gained a particular status as truth, classifiable as perversion and lumped in the same category as those considered to be abnormal or criminals (Signorile, 1997:45). As Bryson (1998) claims:

> Inverts, perverts, abnormal, sick, queer, criminal. You can learn a lot about people from their labels. Some of the pejorative terms of the last several centuries used to describe homosexual behaviour have disappeared. But what these words have in common is that they describe a perversion from the norm—obviously, whatever it is they are describing is on the *outside*. It can therefore be argued that the development of a specific lesbian

and gay culture was originally oppositional to a norm which is
assumed to be biologically "natural," that of "heterosexuality."

Bergling (2001) provides evidence of traces of this discourse of the
repudiation of effeminacy as a disavowal of emasculation on the part
of gay men. Jay, a twenty-one-year-old student from Virginia, states,
for example, "If you want a man you should act like a man," and Gary,
a forty-nine-year-old teacher in Portland, Oregan, who claims to have
been very effeminate when he was younger, was taunted and humili-
ated at the hands of his peers, leading him to join the military at age
eighteen to "reclaim" his masculinity (p. 38). Bergling claims that at
the heart of such responses is a deep-seated form of sexism that
"places men way up *here* and women way down *there*" (p. 58) in a
male-dominated society which explains the strong correlation that he
finds "between negative feelings about women and negative feelings
about effeminate men, especially among those who identify as straight
acting" (p. 60) (see also Simpson, 2003a). Thus, corporeal masculinity emerges as the linchpin for many gay men with a normative force
of performativity that appears to signify a disavowal of the abnormal
and the perverse that historically constituted the gay male as a woman
in a man's body.

Signorile (1997), however, highlights that a particular fashioning
of the gay male body as the "shaved muscle boy aesthetic" is omnipresent in gay men's lives and propagated by the porn industry and
other media technologies from within the gay community to market
the sexed body according to the dictates of particular aestheticized
and eroticized normative ideals:

> These images are played back to us again and again in gay porn,
> on safe sex posters, and in dozens of gay newspapers and several
> glossy national magazines that often sport pumped up cover-
> boys and fetching ads selling products and events, from under-
> wear to hot parties. (p. 25)

Although not all the bodies are necessarily represented as "pumped,"
a particular look or image gets marketed within the limits of regulatory schemas for fashioning the idealized gay male body. These are
compelled by norms for producing desire that centers on penis size
and techniques for enacting gay sex. Within the technologies of cor-
porate consumerism that target the pink dollar, what is produced is

not only an increasingly intensified and "commodified masculine self-consiousness" (Simpson, 2003b), but a normalization of gay sexuality and desire with its capacity to induce anxiety about not measuring up in terms of having the right of kind of body and at least an eight-inch penis. It is in this sense that the porn and media industries targeting gay male sexuality and masculinity need to be thought of as "apparatuses of thought and action" that compel a certain "heterogeneous assemblage of bodies, vocabularies, judgements, techniques, inscriptions, practices" for understanding the subjectification of gay men (Rose, 1996:182). It is in this sense that gay magazines and porn films function as "gender manuals, maps and bibles" (Simpson, 2003b) for inscribing desire and sexual practices for gay men. As Rose argues, what we need to analyze and focus on is how a particular "body regime" has been produced. For gay men, a certain "regime of corporeality" which induces "a certain relation to ourselves as embodied" male subjects is made possible through the deployment of cultural technologies such as the media and the Internet that serve as a means by which certain enunciative regimes are operationalized for composing and deciphering the limits of gay sexuality and modes of relating and desiring as gay men. What gets authorized through such cultural technologies are certain norms that proscribe the limits of the corporeal sex-gender practices through which it is possible to understand our desire. It is in this sense, as Rose (1996:186) argues, that "bodies are always 'thought bodies' or 'bodies-thought.'"

There is a need then to develop interpretive frameworks that enable us to understand the practices of normativity and, hence, technologies of subjectification that incite particular modes of relating to the self. Thus the roles of the media, the Internet, the porn industry, and the urban gay ghetto with its bathhouses, function as significant cultural technologies and disciplinary sites for inciting certain practices of subjectification for gay men through which particular relations to the self are made possible in specific locales:

> Technologies of subjectification, then, are machinations, the being assembled together with particular intellectual and practical instruments, components, entities, and devices that produce certain ways of being human, territorialize, stratify, fix, organize, and render durable particular relations that humans truthfully establish with themselves. (Rose, 1996:186)

The role that the media, the porn industry, and technologies of advertising play in the assemblage and installing of specific norms that incite certain techniques of subjectification and regimes of corporeality in gay men's lives cannot be denied. It is in this sense that we articulate a caution and draw attention to a particular problematics in this book around the constitution of the porn industry or public sex as potential sites for transformation and sexual liberation (see Dowsett, 1996; Warner, 1999). Rather, we argue, here, that it is much more productive to interrogate the technologies of subjectification that govern the assemblage of norms and the logics of practice within specific locales and across particular disciplinary sites that produce a grid of intelligibility for determining and understanding the limits of gay men's modes of relating and acting on sexual desire.

SEXUAL FREEDOM OR SEXUAL OPPRESSION?

Take the following scene. It is an account of an event narrated to one of the authors at a café in Oxford Street, Sydney, by Pierre, the French friend of a friend who is visiting Sydney for the first time. He is a gay man who loves to tell an audience about his encounters, or rather misadventures, with gay men in the gay ghetto of Sydney, always tinged with humor and a sense of wit. But the story he tells on that day took on a particular significance that has never been erased and which continues to resurface four years later—leaving an indelible imprint of a nightmarish scene of sexual oppression, one that is masked, elided, or even denied under the banner of sexual liberation.

> Late at night at a bathhouse. It is dark and Pierre notices a group of men standing around a cubicle with the door left ajar. He joins the spectacle—the collective gay male gaze is turned on the act of two men having sex. One man is Caucasian, he is well built and is standing behind an Asian gay man with long fair hair who is facing the wall. He is fucking him from behind and tugging on his long blond hair with each pelvic thrust. Once it is over, the men disperse but without failing to notice the blood that is trickling slowly down the Asian man's legs. The story is told with humor. It is meant to be funny!

In this book, *Gendered Outcasts and Sexual Outlaws,* the contributors explore further the impact and effects of sexual oppression and power relationships among gay men—social relations that are often racialized, genderized, and eroticized within the porn industry but which get taken up under the banner of sexual liberation and transformative practices of sexual subjectification. The positioning of the sexualized and gendered gay male subject as outcast looms large within the queer community that haunts the very attempts to secure the borders of corporeal masculinity outside of which the "unlivable," "unnarrativizable" self or feminized other can never fully be expunged or expelled. Thus, this book aims to bring together a collection of essays by gay men, all of whom ask gay men to reevaluate what being gay means, why being gay is deemed socially unacceptable, and how we, as a community, respond to systemic stigmatization and hate. The authors share a common belief that gay men need to reexamine what we are saying to one another about appropriate gay male identity and sexuality. Concerned with the rise of sexualized hypermasculinity, racism, and femiphobia within the gay male community, the authors query whether the identity politics gay men are presently advocating is a positive and effective challenge to homophobia and systemic inequality or simply another medium through which to sustain male gender privilege and the harms that result from gender hierarchies. If the latter, what are the harms that result and how are these presently manifesting themselves within the gay male community?

As already reiterated, important issues are raised in this book about the need to explore the effects of normalizing practices in gay men's lives in terms of how they negotiate and perform their masculinities (Simpson, 1994; Martino, 2000). The valorization of particular forms of masculinity is signaled by gay men through language such as "straight-acting" and "gym-toned body," which feeds into a hierarchical gender system that informs the regulation of desire and the policing of gender relations among gay men. The effects of such practices need to be understood within the context of a heteronormative appropriation of a gender system which is problematic in terms of perpetuating a normative ideology of male superiority driven by a denigration and rejection of the feminine (see Bergling, 2001). Those gay men considered to be "girlie" or the least masculine are often devalued in this system of gender relations which is about the production of what Kendall (2001) terms "masculine mimicry" and what Bergling has has referred to as "sissyphobia." The effects of such social practices of masculinity need to be examined in terms of some gay men's investment in particular forms of problematic, hierarchical, and gendered power relationships (see Alvear, 2003).

Many feminist writers have described in detail the links between homophobia and sexism. For these women, to talk of sex discrimination is to talk of gender and the inequalities that arise within a society in which gender differences are polarized and hierarchical—a society in which those who are "male" get privilege and those who are not, do not. In this regard, biology is not a biological attribute, but rather gender as socially constructed and as defined by specific behaviors that ultimately result in the genders "male" and "female." As legal feminist, Catharine MacKinnon (1989:114), explains:

> Gender is an inequality, a social and political concept, a social status based on who is permitted to do what to whom. Male is a social and political concept, not a biological attribute, having nothing whatever to do with inherence, pre-existence, nature, essence, inevitability, or body as such.

It is this social definition of male and female, with defining and rigidly enforced characteristics for each, that ultimately results in gender inequality. In order to reap the benefits awarded to those who are "male" in our society, one must worship and be all that is masculine, that is, a socially constructed set of behaviors and ideas that ultimately define who belongs to the male gender class and that determine who gets and maintains the power commensurate with male gender privilege.

Under this system, "masculinity is seen as the authentic and natural exercise of male agency; femininity as the authentic and natural exercise of female agency" (Franke, 1995:4). To subscribe to masculinity, and to benefit from the privilege afforded "real" men, however, one must *also* support compulsory heterosexuality—an ideology and political institution that embodies those socially defined sets of behaviors and characteristics that ensure heterosexual male dominance and that result in sexual inequality. In this sense then, gender (a system of social hierarchy, an inequality) and sexuality (through which the desire for gender is constantly reproduced) become inseparable.

As MacKinnon again notes, within a system of gender polarity in which male equals dominance, female submission,

> the ruling norms of sexual attraction and expression are fused with gender identity and formation and affirmation, such that sexuality equals heterosexuality equals the sexuality of (male) dominance and (female) submission. . . . Sexuality becomes, in this view, social and relational, constructing and constructed of power. (1989:131, 151)

Heterosexuality must thus be enforced, made compulsory (Rich, 1980), because it is deemed necessary to ensure the survival of both masculinity and femininity, defined as male over female, through which male dominance over women is ensured. Lesbians and gay men potentially challenge this requirement because they can be seen to deny the inevitability of heterosexuality. As such, they are viewed as a threat to male supremacy that must be silenced. As MacKinnon explains, sexuality constructs men as superior to women, ensuring that gender remains hierarchical, ensuring that heterosexuality remains the norm through which gender inequality is maintained, requiring that those who challenge those norms through which gender remains polarized are penalized for nonconformity:

> Sexuality then is a form of power. Gender, as socially constructed, embodies it, not the reverse. Women and men are divided by gender, made into the sexes as we know them, by the social requirements of its dominant form, heterosexuality, which institutionalizes male sexual dominance and female sexual submission. If this is true, sexuality is the linchpin of sexual inequality. (1989:118)

Once we see the extent to which heterosexuality, made compulsory, ensures the maintenance of gender as a system of dominance and submission, of sexual hierarchy, we can begin to see the extent to which antigay stereotypes play into and undergird sex inequality. Together, sexuality and gender form the basis of institutionalized sexism. Sexuality, as constructed, represents the normative ideology of male superiority over women, and the hostility directed at lesbians and gay men finds its source in this power structure, aimed as it is at preserving compulsory heterosexuality.

Building on this work, some gay male writers have queried the effects of what some describe as the gay male community's present obsession with hypermasculinity. Specifically, it has been argued that something has gone terribly wrong with gay male liberation (Stoltenberg, 1989; Kendall, 1999, 2004). The notion of empowerment, of encouraging a self-confidence that ultimately leads to the public expression of dissent and the rejection of those values that daily result in all that is antigay, has been replaced with a selfish, misguided commitment to male dominance and the right to overpower. Equality, in the form of compassion, mutual trust, and respect, has been abandoned for a community ethic and identity politic that encourages and promotes the very essence of inequality: hypermasculinity and the harms that arise from a system in which gender is polarized such that "male" equals top, equals power (Kendall, 2001).

For gay men who have always been ridiculed and abused for their perceived failure to achieve the hypermasculine ideal, the power offered from masculine conformity, although initially appealing, is both a facade and politically myopic. The result is a gay male liberation committed to hierarchy and the inequality, including gay male inequality, that results from heterosexual male dominance and the power that sustains it—a movement committed more to the idea of being "men," socially defined, than to challenging those character traits and enforced gender stereotypes that have always been the source of our inequality and which will continue to result in the suppression of any discourse which strives to validate our right to be gay.

In this chapter, our aim has been to set the stage for questioning the prevalence of a queer politics from within the community that is committed to attacking the "dominant notion of the natural." Rather, what surfaces across many queer social sites and gay male locales, as well as through the deployment of the apparatus of the media and the porn industry, is the mobilization of specific norms for inscribing the limits of sexual desire and practices of corporeal masculinity. These "thought bodies" take on a particular significance within regimes of normalization that compel the force of lived realities of gender hierarchies and sexual oppression at the heart of which always looms the gendered outcast.

REFERENCES

Alvear, M. (2003). *Men are pigs, but we love bacon.* New York: Kensington Books.

Bergling, T. (2001). *Sissyphobia: Gay men and effeminate behavior.* Binghamton, NY: Harrington Park Press.

Bryson, K. (1998). Festival of the inverts: The case for minority representation, *Filmwaves,* Issue 3. Available at <http://www.filmwaves.co.uk/Filmwaves_files/01_14/3gayles. htm>.

Butler, J. (1993). *Bodies that matter: On the discursive limits of sex.* London: Routledge.

Case, Sue-Ellen (1993). Tracking the vampire. *Journal of Feminist Cultural Studies, 3*(2):1-20.

Dowsett, G. (1996). *Practising desire: Homosexual sex in the era of AIDS.* Stanford, CA: Stanford University Press.

Franke, K. (1995). The central mistake of sex discrimination law: The disaggregation of sex from gender. *University of Pennsylvania Law Review, 5:* 1-63.

Kendall, C. (1999). Gay male pornography/gay male community: Power without consent, mimicry without subversion. In J. Kuypers (Ed.), *Men and power* (pp. 86-105). Halifax, Nova Scotia: Fernwood Press.

Kendall, C. (2001). The harms of gay male pornography: A sex equality perspective post Little Sisters Book and Art Emporium. *Gay and Lesbian Law Journal, 2:* 1-36.

Kendall, C. (2004). *Gay male pornography: An issue of sex discrimination.* Vancouver: UBC Press.

Levine, M. (2004), *Gay macho: The life and death of the sexual clone.* New York: NYU Press.

MacKinnon, C. (1989). *Toward a feminist theory of the state.* Cambridge, MA: Harvard University Press.

Martino, W. (2000). Policing masculinities: Investigating the role of homophobia and heteronormativity in the lives of adolescent boys at school. *The Journal of Men's Studies, 8*(2):213-236.

Rich, A. (1980). Compulsory heterosexuality and lesbian experience. *Signs, 54:* 631-660.

Rose, N. (1996). *Inventing ourselves: Psychology, power and personhood.* Cambridge, UK: Cambridge University Press.

Signorile, M. (1997). *Life outside.* New York: Harper Perennial.

Simpson, M. (1994). *Male impersonators: Men performing masculinity.* New York: Routledge.

Simpson, M. (2003a). Fannyphobia. In M. Simpson, *Sex terror: Erotic misadventures in pop culture* (pp. 89-92). Binghamton, NY: Harrington Park Press.

Simpson, M. (2003b). Metrosexual? That rings a bell . . . Available at <http://www.marksimpson.com/pages/journalism/metrosexual_ios.html>.

Simpson, M. (2004). MetroDaddy speaks! Available at <http://www.marksimpson.
    com/pages/journalism/metrodaddyspeaks.html>.
Stoltenberg, J. (1989). *Refusing to be a man: Essays on sex and justice.* New York:
    Meridian.
Warner, M. (1999). *The trouble with normal: Sex politics, and the ethics of queer
    life.* New York: The Free Press.

Chapter 2

Brettles

John Gascoigne

He moved like
Old-style movie glamor
Dewdrops quivered
On the end of eyelashes
Colored like a
Doe with fawn-colored eyes
Pursed lips; he talks
Like a girl I
Noticed him walking.

He wanted me
Tressed up in pigtails
Baby bird in blue
A field of spun sugar hair
Still bristles
On tanned sapling wrists
Slim but muscular; he is
Still a man
Noticed him walking.

Like a gorgeous
Constant camera frame
You move on film
Unbroken—
Your face a mass of
Small movement,
Small beautiful insects
Working in your nerves—
I noticed him walking.

Chapter 3

The Relevance of Radical Feminism for Gay Men

Robert Jensen

I am sexually homeless.

By that I do not mean I am confused about my sexuality, though my sexual desire has meandered all over the map and at various times I have wondered (as, I suspect, most people do at some point in their lives), "Just what the hell am I?" But, at forty-five years of age, I have a reasonably clear sense of that map and the terrain I cover: I sometimes find myself attracted to men, other times to women. I am gay, except when I am straight. Call me bisexual if you like, though it is not how I identify myself. My sexual self-description is I feel straight when I am with a woman and I feel gay when I am with a man. And during periods of celibacy, I bounce between the two.

Instead, my sense of homelessness grows out of the intersection of my sexuality and my politics. I came to understand my gayness through radical feminism (e.g., Frye, 1983) and, more specifically, through the radical feminist critique of pornography (Dworkin, 1988; MacKinnon & Dworkin, 1997). At the same time I was engaging those political philosophies and issues, I also was working through personal questions about my sexuality. The political analysis, which highlighted the construction of sexuality and the power dynamics behind it, helped me to understand the personal in a new way, allowing me to move from being trapped in a conventional heterosexual life to a place where I could acknowledge and begin to express my desire for men. Once those things became clear to me, I felt the understandable sense of liberation, of hope for charting a new path that could combine my sexuality, sexual politics, and radical politics more generally. Nearly a decade later, my short-term optimism (though not necessarily my long-term hope) has mostly evaporated, primarily because I have found no community in which my sexuality and politics easily fit, except perhaps for the radical lesbian feminist community. That is the irony of it all—the source of the ideas that have so helped me understand myself is unavailable to me as a location in which to live. I have learned from radical lesbian feminism and have worked on intellectual and political projects with lesbian feminists, all to my benefit. But men simply cannot be part of some aspects of that community's social and sexual life.

This claim that I am sexually homeless does not mean that I cannot find anyone with whom I can share intimate, philosophical, or political connections. I am fortunate to have close friends with whom I have had a variety of relationships. I am not complaining that "nobody likes me" or "I cannot find a date." I am surrounded by a number of people—gay and straight, men and women—whom I consider to be quite remarkable. I often meet individuals to whom I feel attracted and with whom I can imagine being intimate. I am fortunate to have an active professional and political life that provides satisfaction and a sense of accomplishment. If I were to continue in my current partnerless state indefinitely, I would not consider it a tragedy.

What concerns me most is not my own particular state of being at the moment but, rather, the state of the world. The fact that I can find no community in which I feel at home, in which I can integrate my sexuality, sense of self, and political orientation should be of no interest to others except for what it says about the wider culture. If I were to meet the man and/or woman of my dreams tomorrow, this question of community remains. Consequently, the objective for me—indeed, for all of us—should not simply be finding that "special someone" but, rather, helping to build such a community based (for me) on principles of justice and equality as understood in a radical framework.

Let me expand on my conception of sexuality and sexual politics. The radical feminist analysis in which my ideas are rooted identifies sexual activity as one of the key sites of the oppression of women by men. In patriarchy, sex is based on a dynamic of domination and subordination. Men, generally, are trained through a variety of cultural institutions to view sex as the acquisition of pleasure by the taking of women. Sex is a sphere in which men are trained to see themselves as naturally dominant and women naturally passive. Women are objectified and women's sexuality is commodified. Sex is sexy because men are dominant and women are subordinate; power is conceptualized as erotic. The predictable result is a world in which violence, sexual violence, sexualized violence, and violence-by-sex are so common that they must be considered normal, as expressions of the sexual norms of the culture, rather than violations of those norms.

The foundation of this routine fusing of sexuality and various levels of violence is men's power over women, but in patriarchy other disparities of power such as race and ethnicity can be, and routinely are, sexualized. Power dynamics can be created—tops and bottoms, masculine and feminine—within same-sex relationships, even when the participants are of relatively equal status. The fact that people may move between those roles (that is, a man can be both a top and a bottom in a relationship) does nothing to undermine the existence of the roles and the power dynamic of which they are a part. Instead of eroticizing power, the radical feminist critique challenges us to eroticize equality.

Although we should work to eliminate the differences in power that stem from illegitimate authority such as sexism and racism, there is no way to equalize all differences in power that emerge because of people's differing talents and temperaments in specific situations (and, in fact, attempting to eliminate those differences would be disastrous). So, there will always be complex questions about power, even when people consciously work at establishing egalitarian relationships. The goal is not some totalitarian imposition of rules but a constant awareness of how power differences are routinely sexualized and how that affects relationships. The task is to engage in critical self-reflection about the way those power relations affect the most intimate aspects of our lives and ask if there are not other ways to structure our lives that will be more satisfying.

Understanding the role that power plays in sexuality is a complex endeavor; however, some integral components of that understanding are fairly straightforward. I believe that a fundamental tenet of a progressive sexual ethic is that people and their sexuality should not be bought and sold, that intimacy is not a commodity for the market. This assertion is based on a principle of justice and a sense of empathy, growing out of a conception of what I believe human beings are for and a concern for those who are routinely and predictably hurt in such a system. That same sense of justice and empathy leads me to oppose capitalism more generally, again for that simple reason: People are people, not things to be used by others.

But to remain focused on sexuality: If intimacy is an arena in which people have maximal freedom to explore themselves and others in relatively egalitarian relationships, sexuality can be a source of liberation. If intimacy is an arena in which people's erotic experiences are structured by dynamics of domination and subordination, sexuality will be a tool of control. Buying a person for sex is domination; in a world based on equality, sex would not be a commodity.

I am aware that some individuals clearly state they want to offer themselves and their sexuality for sale, whether it is in prostitution, pornography, strip bars, or other aspects of the sex industry (Delacoste & Alexander, 1998). I am not contesting their capacity to make such a decision. Instead, I am arguing for a different sexual ethic. My goal is not to harangue those who make that choice but instead to be part of a movement that tries to change the society so that the sex industry becomes obsolete. My goal is not to impose my sexual ethic on others but to explain why I think a radical feminist critique is compelling and why the norms of the society should change.

I am aware that gay pornography has been one of the few sites where gay youth have been able to see representations of same-sex love and gay men have been able to see their desire for men validated. But that fact does not constitute an argument for why we must continue to accept a practice or tradition rather than seek new, and perhaps better, ways to achieve that result. I am not against the exploration of sexuality through art and literature but, instead, am arguing against the way in which the pornography industry uses people to create profit, and not a deeper understanding of sexuality.

People often defend pornography, straight or gay, with the claim that it frees up people's sexual imaginations. I argue the opposite: pornography tends to limit our imaginations, forcing sexuality into channels that typically reproduce a domination/subordination dynamic. I am suggesting we should reject the commercialization and objectification inherent in the sex industry and look for new ways to validate gay sexuality.

This argument brings me back to my homelessness. I have met some men who are interested in these kinds of questions and this kind of analysis, and are willing to talk about it. But I have found very few gay men who are interested in this as a *political project*. That is, I have not met many gay men who are willing to publicly identify with (or sometimes even engage in) the radical feminist critique, and use that framework to analyze gay culture.

Let me be clear: By arguing this position I am not accepting the hackneyed stereotype that all gay men are promiscuous, bar-hopping, bathhouse dwellers. Certainly that stereotype describes some percentage of the gay male world, and I think the radical feminist critique offers a way for gay men to critique those practices. But just as certainly many gay men are involved in what the straight world would consider (if not for the same-sex partner) conventional relationships, and that same radical feminist analysis also offers a way for us to critique some aspects of those relationships. But significant space for a political and cultural project rooted in radical feminism or a radical politics more generally has not opened up in contemporary gay male culture. In my experience, there is virtually no public critique of pornography and, more generally, the sex industry in the gay male world. To the degree that critical discussion takes place about promiscuity and the practice of anonymous sex, it is rooted mostly in conservative reaction against the "homosexual lifestyle." In my experience, most gay men consider these issues to be matters of personal preference and not politics. Again, I am not arguing that gay men refrain from thinking or talking about such things, but that those discussions are conducted largely in private and rarely as part of a coherent political project rooted in an egalitarian ethic. The discussion among gay men that goes on in public is largely a contest between a sex liberal/libertarian position and those who want to see gay men fit into the existing heterosexual system. There are some notable exceptions to this, such as the work of Christopher Kendall (1995) and John Stoltenberg (2000), but I think this quick sketch is a reasonable account of the main currents in the culture.

Why is it the case that gay male culture seems to be invested in sexual objectification and commodification to a degree at least as intense as its heterosexual counterpart? The simple answer is that being gay does not automatically mean a rejection of patriarchy, its sexual ethic, or its values. The struggle against patriarchy is a political struggle, one in which people must make a choice to resist. For men, gay or straight, that means a choice to resist a system that in various ways gives us privilege. To recognize that gay men are discriminated against in society in some ways should not keep us from seeing the ways that they retain privileges as men.

Of course, the feminist analysis in which I am rooted is but one approach to gender and sexuality. Other men, gay and straight, may endorse other feminist analyses (including some that celebrate pornography and the sex industry) and may contend that they are just as committed to the end of patriarchy. I am not suggesting all other political positions are illegitimate but instead am making a case for the one I find most compelling; I believe it accounts for the evidence in an intellectually and morally honest fashion. It confronts difficult truths and offers a politics with integrity. Given the abbreviated nature of this essay, I am not attempting a thorough defense of the radical feminist analysis nor its relevance to gay life and politics. Instead, I am sketching my own alienation from gay politics and culture, perhaps with the hope that others, who see some aspect of their own experience reflected in these comments, will be motivated to look further into the work of these feminists.

After completing a book on heterosexual pornography a few years ago, I gave some thought to undertaking a similar project on gay pornography. I did not pursue it. One reason was because my intellectual and political interests were increasingly centered on understanding and resisting the threat to the people of the developing world posed by the militarism and greed of the U.S. government and the corporations that set its agenda. What time I allocate to other projects tends to focus on sexism and racism, places where as a white man I think I have compelling moral obligations. I return regularly to the feminist critique, issues of the sex industry, and the project of resisting patriarchy in part because I continue to believe the issues are important and also because I think that resistance is integral to my other political interests. Eroding the power of patriarchy will help in the struggle against militarism, capitalism, and racism.

But the decision to focus on other work also had to do with an assessment of what seemed possible at that moment in gay culture. I wish I saw more signs that these interests could find a home there, but for now I do not. However, I believe that over time the value of radical feminism's resistance to patriarchy will become clearer to gay men. Although it often seems more "realistic" politically for marginalized groups to work to carve out a space in the dominant society rather than challenge the fundamental patriarchal norms of that society, I think such an approach is dangerous. One makes many compromises in political struggles, and dogmatic assertions of political purity are mostly self-indulgent. But there is a great difference between making judgments about short-term compromises with an unjust system to advance a political project, and accepting without question the unjust norms and principles on which the system is based. I believe that in the long run, a gay rights movement that accepts the norms of commodification and objectification in capitalism and patriarchy will flounder. The future—if it is to be a decent one—lies in a consistent rejection of a world structured on domination, from the most intimate parts of our lives to the largest questions of global justice.

REFERENCES

Delacoste, F. & Alexander, P. (1998). *Sex work* (2nd ed.). San Francisco, CA: Cleis Press.

Dworkin, A. (1988). *Letters from a war zone.* New York: Dutton.

Frye, M. (1983). *The politics of reality: Essays in feminist theory.* Freedom, CA: Crossing Press.

Kendall, C. (1995). Gay male pornography and the sexualization of masculine identity. In L. Lederer & R. Delgado (Eds.), *The price we pay: The case against racist speech, hate propaganda and pornography* (pp. 102-122). New York: Farrar, Strauss & Giroux.

MacKinnon, C., & Dworkin, A. (1997). *In harm's way: The pornography civil rights hearings.* Cambridge, MA: Harvard University Press.

Stoltenberg, J. (2000). *Refusing to be a man: Essays on sex and justice.* New York: Routledge.

Chapter 4

Sissyphobia and Everything After

Tim Bergling

"It is with a painful eye, I remember seeing things Adam did that looked 'so gay' during his high school years when we were keeping the gay issue in the family closet," the mother wrote in her e-mail. "I wanted to tell him so that he could correct it and no one would know our secret. I also remember when he started to wear those tight shirts; I asked him one morning 'Adam, why don't you wear a sign on your back saying, "I am gay."'" (That went over like a lead balloon.) If I accept my son's sexuality why do I care if he is effeminate or not? Would I risk hurting his self-esteem by bringing these things to his attention?

"As a parent unconditional love gets overcome with fear. However, I do feel that Adam has our unconditional love . . . I just like to offer a few suggestions every now and then . . . Thanks for the book. *Sissyphobia* made me start to question what I feel about effeminate men. I found that my feeling about the guy off the street that is effeminate, and my son being effeminate, requires different scoring cards."

That's just a small excerpt from among the hundreds of e-mails I received after the publication of my book *Sissyphobia: Gay Men and Effeminate Behavior* (Harrington Park Press, 2001), but it's one of a good dozen or so that stand out in my mind. Nothing could be more gratifying for a writer than to hear that his book has had a real effect on someone's life, especially if that effect was to bring a mother somehow just a little bit closer to her gay son.

Or a gay man closer to his own feelings when it comes to men less masculine than he. "I used to really, *really* look down on effeminate guys before I read your book," wrote one guy in his midtwenties. "I used to think they liked acting that way, or only acted that way to piss people off. But reading *Sissyphobia* really opened my eyes to what a prejudiced shit I was being. I don't think I'll ever be like that again."

Although I am humbled by that and the other overwhelmingly positive responses I got, I have to admit that trying to effect life changes in my readers wasn't really on my radar screen when I wrote the book, or the 1997 *Genre* magazine article upon which it was based. (That was actually inspired by a long, late-night conversation I had with my straight best friend, who despite his complete comfort with my sexuality, had to admit that "really swishy guys" gave him the creeps.) Nor did I have any idea that I was setting off on a bit of a journey of self-discovery, where my own feelings about effeminate men would be tested countless times.

Both the article and the book were simply intended to satisfy what I found to be an enduring curiosity for me, and for many other gay men. Where *does* effeminate behavior in gay men come from? Why is it that some gay men behave in a stereotypical effeminate—or even flamboyant—manner, while other gay men are undetectable as such from the way they speak or move? To help answer those questions, I contacted various geneticists, sociologists, activists, and other experts to get their take on the biological and social theories of effeminate behavior's origins, as well as the origin of same-sex orientation itself. I found there are no "right" answers, but rather many schools of thought, some of them quite opposed to one another. I tried to represent each as faithfully as I could.

But although those theories are fascinating, they represent the smaller portion of the book. The much larger issue is the phenomenon I came to call "sissyphobia": not *homo*phobia, which is usually defined as a hatred or fear of gays and lesbians by straight people, but the hatred, fear, or just distaste that straight *and* gay people have for a man who behaves in an effeminate way. I wanted to know what it is about effeminate behavior that riles so many in our community and the straight world outside. Or turning that question around: What is it about our society that has such a problem with men who behave in an effeminate manner?

As I began my research I became amazed at the lack of material that had been specifically published on the topic up to that time. This, after all, is the single phenomenon that sets gay males apart in the company of their straight counterparts in school hallways, locker rooms, the workplace, or out on the street. This is our "fag tag," if you will, the combination of motion and speech straight guys imitate when ridiculing us, or even referencing us good-naturedly. One would imagine there'd be scores of writings for me to devour and draw from. And yet—except for a very few academic works—I found almost nothing. (Even the academics weren't much help. The head of one university Queer Studies department told me he didn't see where society necessarily equated a limp wrist or lisping speech with homosexuality, leading me to conclude that he'd been spending way too much time high up in his ivory tower and not enough time down here in the real world.)

So I devised a survey, sending it out to hundreds of people I met in online chat rooms, out at the bars, and a dozen other places. I scanned hundreds of personal ads culled from gay newspapers and publications from all over the country, logging every reference made to men who behaved in a "less than manly" manner. And I posted notices about the book on various online bulletin boards, soliciting any comment on effeminate men that "regular" folks might care to make.

Soon enough, reactions started streaming in, some of them surprising. Many men had severely negative reactions to the project itself. "You're going to write about *that?*" they'd ask me, aghast at the prospect of my shining a spotlight on the fairer portion of our same-sex set. "Why bring all that up and give straight men even more ammunition against us?" (As if straight men needed a nudge from *me* to notice the obviously gay men in their midst.) It became clear rather quickly that for lots of us, especially those involved in gay rights activism, the topic of effeminate behavior is rather like the dead body of a big pink elephant splayed out in the middle of the room: something pretty hard to ignore, yet a topic many of us are politely stepping around without making too much of a fuss about.

Note I said *most* of us. It didn't take much prodding to get other gay men to sound off. "I think effeminate guys are ok and I have some friends that are like that, but I wouldn't want to date one 'cause every time they open their mouths in intimate conversation I just wanna beat their faces in," wrote one young man, who noted that he was "straight acting" and quite proud of it. "Gay society has been stereotyped by this type of behavior which makes me sick . . . I just wish some people wouldn't stereotype my lifestyle off of some faggoty-ass queen in a pink jumpsuit on rollerblades blowing bubbles at gay pride."

Still others got in touch with me to let me know they were not in the least ashamed of their femme sides and were quite happy to puncture what they saw as utter hypocrisy in their straight-acting brethren. "These are boys who like to play with boys, right?" asked one man rhetorically. "Well, how 'straight acting' exactly are you being, when you've got some guy's dick in your mouth?"

I suspected from the start this might be a fertile field to plow, but I wasn't really prepared for the depth of emotion I was going to encounter. I certainly found a number of men for whom effeminate behavior was a complete nonissue, and others who found it engaging or attractive. But they were a minority. Most gay men appeared to have adopted a "two tribe" mentality that splits the gay community into an "us" and a "them." This led me to wonder then—and wonder still—how we can ever expect the straight world outside to ever accept any of us if we can't learn to embrace the diversity within our own ranks.

But documenting the negative opinions that some gay men have for men they deem less manly—and giving voice to the equally strong reaction of the other tribe—was actually the easiest part of the whole exercise. Anyone who has ever picked up a gay men's magazine has known forever the adoration that most gay men seem to have for masculine —i.e., "straight-acting"—men, and a general loathing of those who were not. It was a bit thornier to actually pinpoint the *origins* of effeminate behavior and to find the root of the hostility often aimed at men who behave in such a way; still, after dozens of interviews and scores of questions aimed at experts in their fields of study, and "regular" gay men of all stripes, I think I have some answers. (If you haven't read *Sissyphobia* yet, and you'd like to see the results of what I found in their full telling, stop reading this *right now.* Otherwise a much briefer synthesis follows.)

To answer the question "where does effeminate behavior come from?" largely depends on where you believe homosexuality *itself* originates. If you happen to belong to what's commonly referred to as the "social constructionist" school, which subscribes to a belief that we all create our sense of gender and sexuality from the information we receive from countless social sources, and then begin to express as we mature, the very question is moot or meaningless. We're gay because we've created that identity for ourselves, and the so-called effeminate expression of that identity is simply part and parcel of who we are. A large number of academics and sociologists hold firm to this belief; they take great issue with the biologists and geneticists who argue an entirely different theory; to wit, that we're gay because we're biologically programmed as such.

That's referred to as the "essentialist" view, that we're essentially born gay, straight, or somewhere in between, through some interaction of genes and hormones in the womb. This view still makes room for a social impact on how we express ourselves, whether we choose to bury our homosexuality because of our environment or to "come out" to varying degrees as we grow up. But the idea here is that human sexuality, though fluid to a small degree depending on social circumstance, is largely hardwired by our very biology and not much subject to change.

The essentialist view also has what I find to be a persuasive answer to questions of effeminate behavior. Boys who exhibit effeminate tendencies from an early age are often subject to extremely cruel treatment at the hands of their peers and even their families; *Sissyphobia* documents several such instances in full, heartbreaking detail. Because it is within the nature of most of us to conform to some degree in order to fit in as best we can, it just seemed somewhat logical to me to believe that some kind of imperative might be at work here, something that for some men makes their effeminate behavior something nearly immutable. And science had an answer here that social constructionists did not. The essentialist theory describes a certain biological process at work in the sexual development of the brain, where levels of sexual orientation are often inextricably linked with sexual characteristics honed over a million years of evolution. Not *always,* mind you; the brain is more complicated than we can possibly imagine, and when you add human social constructs to the mix the full variety of orientation and behavior are myriad. Boiled down though, it became rather obvious to me that most gay men who behave in an effeminate way are simply being themselves, just as any gay man—masculine or effeminate—who indulges his true sexual nature is being himself as well.

This is a key point, because it sets up the more bothersome topic of society's responses to that behavior. Why do so many of us, gay or straight, have a problem when men are "less than manly"? And how can gay men, themselves the frequent object of hostility from heterosexual society, justify their own disdain or outright revulsion for their own brothers, even if they behave more like sisters?

Again, at the risk of oversimplifying my results, here's what I found. First, most "straight-acting" gay men—and that *is* a phrase that calls for quotation marks, self-contradiction that it is—tend to prize masculinity. That being the case, they do not much like being "tarred with the big pink brush" of effeminate behavior; they don't want to be linked with such men in the hearts and minds of friends and family. They don't like the fact that, for most straight people, gay equals sissy, and they resent effeminate men for perpetuating the stereotype. They hate the idea that other people might presume that their naturally masculine behavior must be a front of sorts to mask a truly "nellie" interior.

Even men who admitted having certain effeminate characteristics themselves rarely expressed any attraction or admiration for such men; "I can't date anyone more glam than I am" was how one put it to me. All this begs the question of how such behavior has become such an enduring source of so much opprobrium. The answer I came up with through my interviews and surveys is both simple and unsettling; we don't like effeminate behavior much, because our society at large devalues femininity itself. Men are up *here* in the social structure; women are down *there*. Therefore, any man who surrenders his God-given position in the hierarchy to behave in such a womanlike way is worthy of nothing but scorn. I do not claim that all of us feel that way; it's just that, in resenting or reviling effeminate men, we're giving in to an endemic if sometimes subtle social mind-set. I would further submit that, as sexist attitudes of what's "right" and "wrong" for manly and womanly roles and behavior begin to die out over time, so too will those disdainful attitudes about effeminate gay men.

I also took pains, though, to differentiate between the obvious ills of those attitudes and men who simply expressed an *attraction* to men who happened *not* to be effeminate. Throughout the book, I was as honest as I could be about my own hypocrisies and prejudices. For whatever reason, I grew to adulthood with characteristics most gay men would likely describe as "butch"; though I had extreme compassion for all those who told me stories of being teased about their "sissy" behavior for as long as they could remember, I could not admit that effeminate behavior was something I'd ever been much attracted to myself. Although I don't think anyone should ever have to apologize or justify those qualities he finds enticing in someone else—and the things he does *not* find attractive or enticing—I found myself curiously uncomfortable at times relaying all the rather heartless comments some "straight-acting" fellows made about the femme guys. Sometimes I saw too much of myself in their words, which is why I've often described researching and writing the book as something of a journey.

It's a journey that's going on in society at large as well. In the book, I make mention of the many strides gay men had thus far made in the popular consciousness, as well as the world of art and entertainment. Years after *Sissyphobia*, the Bravo network's *Queer Eye for the Straight Guy* has taken television by storm. Five openly gay and variously flamboyant men, schooled in design, culture, and couture, endeavor each week to "make over" a hapless heterosexual's lifestyle. It's a puzzling phenomenon that manages to confirm, deride, and confound stereotypes, and America is eating it up.

And though *Sissyphobia* has long been completed, and I've embarked on several new projects since—a book that explores ageism as it exists in the gay community, another that delves into gay men and how far they're willing to go in the pursuit of "perfection" in themselves and others, and still another on the curious relationship between gay men and lesbians—e-mails and letters on *Sissyphobia* still find their way to me.

"I am so glad someone finally wrote a book about this," one young man wrote just a few months ago. "I used to be one of those guys who was afraid to be himself, always felt like I had to 'butch it up' all the time. Now I see that there's nothing wrong with me being me, and if someone has a problem with it he can just go pound sand up his ass."

Chapter 5

Straight-Acting Masculinities: Normalization and Gender Hierarchies in Gay Men's Lives

Wayne Martino

> . . . the subject is constituted through the force of exclusion and abjection, one which produces a constitutive outside of the subject, an abjected outside, which is, after all, "inside" the subject as its own founding repudiation. (Butler, 1993:3)

INTRODUCTION

In this chapter I want to focus on how "doing masculinity" (Coleman, 1990) impacts in significant ways on how gay men come to understand themselves as particular kinds of gendered subjects and what this means in terms of their expression and articulation of sexual desire for other men. In drawing attention to the impact and effects of the "repudiation of the feminine" as a regulatory mechanism for the policing of masculinities in gay men's lives, I highlight how normalization and gender hierarchies are implicated in the way that some gay men embody their masculinities (Bergling, 2001). In drawing primarily on the work of Butler (1993), Bersani (1995), and Grosz (1995) to emphasize the extent to which the body matters in gay men's lives, I foreground how sexual desire is inextricably tied to a disavowal of the feminine, which is signified and embodied in the constitution of the "feminized faggot" or queen as a despised figure of phantasmatic abjection. Thus, I draw attention to how desire is inscribed through a symbolic order that is implicated in a gender hierarchical system which produces effects at the level of embodied social relations and practices. In this sense, I argue that the body, as a site for the inscription and iteration of particular self-fashioning and performative practices of masculinity, is governed by norms that dictate the negotiation of certain signifying and psychic practices that appear to inform many gay men's appropriation of an idealized hegemonic masculinity at the basis of which lies the "regulatory apparatus of heterosexuality" (Butler, 1993:12; see also Connell, 1992, 1995). The effects of such practices are traced in terms of how straight-acting masculinities get eroticized, embodied, and objectified for some gay men within a heteronormative economy of desire that is built on reinforcing rather than subverting gender hierarchies and oppositional categories.

WHICH BODIES MATTER?
HOMOPHOBIC POLICING OF MASCULINITIES

Butler (1993) raises issues about the constraints imposed by the materialization of sexed bodies within the limits of a grid of cultural intelligibility that is circumscribed through the mobilization of historically contingent norms for fashioning gendered subjectivities. In this regard, she reiterates Foucault's (1984) emphasis on the regulation and policing of sexuality within the context of historically specific power relations and disciplinary apparatuses.

Foucault draws attention to historically contingent modes of subjectification in his genealogical analysis of how sexuality gets constituted and regulated within disciplinary regimens of Christian and Freudian psychoanalytic technologies of self-formation (Foucault 1985, 1986; see also Rose, 1989; Hutton, 1988). Installed within such regimes of self-formation and normalizing practices is the imperative to adopt particular techniques of the self. These constitute capacities for governing and fashioning conduct and specific gendered subjectivities that are formed and maintained over time, but through what Butler (1993) terms a "forcible reiteration" of specific norms. It is in this sense that "sex is a regulatory ideal whose materialization takes place (or fails to take place) through certain highly regulated practices" (Butler, 1993:1).

This raises the issue of the emergence and homophobic policing of masculinities (Martino, 2000) in relation to the materialization of the sexed body and its symbolic significance for some gay men in terms of how they come to understand and articulate their sexual desire and erotic interests for other men (see Bergling, 2001; Burfitt, 1998; Connell, 1992). The following statements, taken from a personals site for gay men, known as straightacting.com,* assume a particular symbolic and performative significance in highlighting how the materialization of the body emerges for these gay men in terms of a specification of gender norms that compels a particular form of "straight-acting" or *normalized* masculinity:

> I am a regular guy who happens to be gay but not attracted to feminine guys and I am a straight-acting guy—I don't act gay cause it's just not me—am looking for a relationship with someone who is comfortable with who they are but still is masculine or straight-acting, but can still love a man and be a man at the same time—not necessarily closeted either—just a "guy." (GM1, age 34, Brooklyn, New York)

> I'm a horny soldier with nothing but my fist to keep me company. I like men who know how to be men. (GM2, age 24, Massachusetts)

> I am very straight-acting (acting feminine is a real turn-off for me) and ideally would like to meet a guy who is the same. (GM3, age 33, Toronto)

> I'm just your everyday normal straight-acting guy next door who just happens to like other everyday straight-acting guys next door . . . I'm a country boy, and love country living. I'm not into the gay scene or drama. I am an outdoors type, love about anything having to do with the outdoors. I'm seeking some much like myself, attractive, honest, straight-acting, 0-say-4 healthy, faithful, between the ages of 24 and 44 at oldest, some one outgoing, kind, exciting, and I tend to like guys who are nice built, no offence but don't like guys who don't take care of themselves or are overweight. Looking for a guy that is wanting a best friend plus life time relationship. (GM4, age 34, Tennessee)

The Web site where these personals are posted has been established especially for those gay males who see themselves as "regular, normal guys"—just men who are sexually attracted to other men.

---

*This is a Web site for gay men "who are more masculine than the effeminate stereotypes." It involves taking a quiz which then enables a score from 1 to 10 to be allocated and which is indicative of the extent to which you rate as a straight-acting gay man (1 is the highest indicator of straight-acting embodied masculinity).

GM1, for example, is searching for a masculine straight-acting man who "can still love a man and be a man at the same time." GM2 is attracted to men who "know how to be men," while GM3 asserts that he is *very* straight-acting, and GM4 is "just your normal, everyday straight-acting guy next door" who is seeking the same. All such assertions are governed by the necessity of these gay men to expel the "feminine other" and exemplify an instance of the "discursive regulation of the boundaries of sexual legitimacy" for these gay men in the articulation of their desire for other men (Butler, 1993:223). In short, the regulatory and normalizing self-fashioning practices of masculinity that are legitimated by many gay men choosing to use this site are illustrated in terms of the constitutive force of exclusion and abjection which cannot be expelled from the symbolic realm that circumscribes the intermeshing of these men's sexual and gendered identities (see Butler, 1993; Harding, 1998; Connell, 2002). Although it could be argued that there is subversive potential in the appropriation of straight-acting masculinities for gay men who defy the mainstream culture's representation and positioning of gay men as the "feminized faggot," the "masculinity confirming" (Renold, 2003) discourses that are mobilized by these men are circumscribed within the regulatory apparatus of heterosexuality that is invested in essentializing, naturalizing, and eroticizing a form of masculine power—a power that is produced through the force of constituting an abjected feminized Other as its "own founding repudiation" (Butler, 1993:3). It is in this sense that the appropriation of straight-acting masculinity constitutes what is termed by Bersani (1995) as the "heterosexualising of homosexuality" (p. 132). What is emphasised and, in fact, reinforced by these men in their assertions are gender hierarchies that circumscribe and limit the articulation and expression of homosexual desire. In this sense, it is a heteronormative economy of desire that gets internalized by these men, one built on reinstating gender binaries and gender hierarchies (see Kaufman, 1999; Stoltenberg, 1989, 1999; Kendall, 1999; Kimmel, 1999; Messner, 1997).

On the straight-acting Web site there are also forums where certain topics for discussion are posted. One of the topics took the form of the following question: *Do you avoid effeminate men?* This question highlights how the straight-acting gay male is haunted by the specter of an abjected, effeminized outside or Other. The "constitutive outside of the subject" can never be erased and is invoked through the iterative self-fashioning practices of masculinity that mark out the boundaries of limits of same-sex desire for these gay men (see Butler, 1993). The following responses are illustrative of this:

> Not to offend anyone, but really effeminate guys' voices/mannerisms tend to grate on my nerves. This one guy in Government, every time he talks, I shudder and die a little more. I guess I would be ok around slightly effeminate guys, but if they open their mouths and a purse falls out, I just can't deal with it. (Straight-acting 1)

> I think part of fear/desire to avoid effeminate men doesn't have anything to do with gayness. Some people are by nature loud-talkers, or just loud, or gesticulate a lot (you know, like Jim Carey) and I think some people in some settings are just embarrassed by the less-than-subdued behavior of these folks. A bit in the same way that some people insist on making "a scene" at a restaurant or anywhere they received [what they see as] less than stellar service (and you just want to sink in your seat, praying that they won't spit in your dessert too). It just so happens that effeminate men (such as the *Queer Eye* guys) have that sort of behavior and are sometimes up in arms (literally!) about little things in daily life. The other is of course "guilt by association." If there's just the two of you and then everyone instantly assumes that he's gay, there's a concern that "people" (using it in the generically dismissive sense of the word) will think of you two as being an item. So in a way, I think there's a fear of being outed (or losing control over who you wish to tell about your sexuality), still I would stop short of saying it's homophobia. (Straight-acting 2)

Straight-acting 2 raises significant issues about the exclusionary and regulatory practices of masculinity in some gay men's lives. He claims that the desire to avoid effeminate men has to do with what appears to be their flamboyant behavior and apparent desire to draw unnecessary attention to themselves (see Bergling, 2001). His explanatory reference to the "*Queer Eye* guys" is significant in highlighting how the media appropriates a particular version of gay masculinity for consumption by mainstream straight culture—queer visibility in the form of the effeminate gay male confirms straight society's representation and normalization of gay men as lacking masculinity. Straight-acting 2's response in this regard is interesting because it highlights the extent to which he rationalizes his rejection of effeminate gay men in terms of the fear of "being outed." It is about "losing control" over the choice to declare one's sexuality. The effeminate gay man functions within a panopticonic regime of surveillance (Foucault, 1977) for identifying an abjected, gay male sexuality that is threatening to straight-acting gay men, whose homosexuality cannot be so easily read off the body. It is this avoidance of being subjected to the gaze of straight society and, hence, made the object of that normalizing practice that appears to motivate this gay man's compulsion to assimilate and to become invisibilized as a gay male subject. However, straight-acting gay men's avoidance of effeminate gay men is rejected as an instance of homophobic dissociation and is framed, in terms of liberal humanist discourses of empowerment, as the right to declare one's sexuality as opposed to being named by association. What this highlights is the ever-haunting presence of the constitutive "outside" of the subject that can never be erased within a sex-gender system supported by the regulatory apparatus of compulsory heterosexuality (see Fuss, 1991).

Another topic of discussion was initiated by a high school student asking for clarification about the meaning of the term "straight-acting":

> . . . I've just been wondering, what really makes a dude "straight-acting" or plain gay? Is it the way he acts, what he sounds like and the way he pronounces the infamous *s?* Or has it more to do with just the personality? I guess it also collides with the question: Is it possible to be out and straight-acting? . . . Haha. I guess you can tell that I'm young and new . . .

Once again the issue of public visibility and identification of gay male sexuality, as embodying a particular form of effeminacy, is raised (see also Martino & Pallotta-Chiarolli, 2003: Chapter 5). Thus being "plain gay" is identified in opposition to the notion of being a straight-acting gay male. The former is associated with the way someone acts or sounds—"the way he pronounces the infamous *s*"—thereby invoking the stereotype of the lisping gay male or feminized faggot. What follows are some of the responses of gay men who offer their own definitions of the term straight-acting:

> Basically it's appearing like everyone else on the street or do people whisper and go "look at that fag" as you walk by. It's actually more of a joke (the term). I only distinguish between what's masculine and what's feminine. Some of us just prefer football and beer to Madonna and the latest fashion craze. (GM1, Florida)

Straight-acting is just a convenient term for masculine . . . The straight-acting gay guy prefers guys to go to bed with and form relationships with—but otherwise is like any old dude walking down the street. (GM2, Sydney)

I've always disliked the term straight-acting. It implies that I'm trying to be something I'm not. I don't find it offensive in any way, I just don't like the wording. I think what we're trying to get at here is just because we're gay, doesn't mean that we wear chiffon and prance around in high heels. We're content to wear flannel, work on our cars, watch sports and do "manly-man" things . . . . I think you will find that most of us here do not define ourselves by our sexuality, and that is a key difference. Approaching life as a "homosexual who happens to be male" will lead to vastly different points of view and behaviors than approaching life as a "male that happens to be homosexual." (GM3, Rochester, New York)

There should be a better word for guys who are guys but just happen to be attracted to other guys. I guess I always knew that being gay didn't mean that I had to be the stereotype. But somehow that stubborn thought just stayed in there to poison the way I think. Oh, and thanks for making me feel welcome; it's really nice to be a part of something where I don't need a facade. (GM4, Miami)

Some guys, and I count myself in this group, are still guys even though they're queer. I've never considered myself "butch," but I do regular guy stuff—run a chainsaw, ride a Harley, work in construction. None of this is for show, it's just because it's fun or it needs to get done. I suppose "butch" could even be used to describe those straight guys who go to exaggerated lengths with cars or trucks or whatever studly stuff to prove to world and to themselves that they're "real" men. Maybe this also the reason for my discomfort with the whole term "straight-acting." I don't want to meet actors. I want to meet men. Butch guys and acting guys need not apply. Am I alone in this? (GM5)

You're definitely not alone, but I don't think the term "straight-acting" is meant to be taken literally. It doesn't mean acting in the Hollywood sense. It describes your actions. You act like a normal guy. It doesn't mean you're covering up something else, or pretending to be a straight guy. I want to meet men also. I want to meet men who act like men because they are men. (GM6, North Carolina)

I know exactly what you mean. I view myself as a normal guy except for the fact that I like men instead of women. (GM7)

The ways in which these men define straight-acting masculinity does highlight the extent to which their practices of self-decipherment are situated within broader regimes of surveillance and monitoring of the limits of the sexed body. In short, what is highlighted is the extent to which straight-acting signifies a particular form of gendered subjectification that is implicated in regimes of normalization and policing of masculinities in gay men's lives. The issue raised by GM5 about his discomfort with the term relates to his rejection of any sense that he is acting or pretending to be someone that he is not—he is merely behaving as a "normal" man should. This is why he rejects the term "butch" because it also implies an act or an exaggerated and, hence, fake replication of masculinity (see also GM3). This is supported by the responses to his posting by GM6 and GM7 who assert that straight-acting is just about being a "normal guy."

These responses support Butler's thesis that the sexed body is pro duced through iterative and citational performative practices that are governed by quite specific norms compelling the signifying and identificatory processes encapsulated by the deployment of the category "straight-acting"

In short, what gets asserted as "normal" or "natural" for many gay men, in terms of expressing their masculinity, needs to be understood as a materialization of the body that takes on the appearance of "normal" as a result of "a forcible reiteration of norms." Hence, the performative practices of gay masculinity may be understood as dictated by "the constrained appropriation of the regulatory law, by the materialization of that law, the compulsory appropriation and identification with those normative demands" (Butler, 1993:12).

While understandably desiring to reject any notion that their straight-acting masculinity is indeed a facade—these men are adamant in their assertions that they are simply "normal, everyday guys" who are not putting on any act. They are just "being themselves," unlike the flaming queens who haunt the policing and embodied practices of their masculinities, understood here as an abjected outside that is manifested in their articulation of gay male desire (GM1 and GM2). What cannot be denied, however, is the extent to which what gets rationalized as "normal" is in fact a "reiterative and citational practice by which discourse produces the effects that it names" (Butler, 1993:2).

It is in this sense that the "normal," understood by these gay men in terms of a particular signification of masculinity, materializes as a particular embodied, self-fashioning, and performative practice. The effect of the iteration of such norms is experienced as a "lived necessity" for these gay men who are compelled by a law of doing masculinity in the service of warding off any attributions of effeminacy that further reinforce the reading of homosexuality as deviant. In this sense, "straight-acting" functions as a compensatory mechanism for displacing an already internalized sense of inferiority that is attributed on the basis of identifying as gay, constituted as failed masculinity. This is realized through the iteration of specific norms that are in the service of reinforcing and rearticulating the hegemonic force of a hierarchical gender binary system, built on a misogynist repudiation and denigration of the feminine. It is in this sense that that these gay men are implicated in a system of sexual oppression and inequality that mimics "the consolidation of the heterosexual imperative" (see Kendall, 1999; Stoltenberg, 1999). This is supported by Bersani (1995) who argues:

> In his desires, the gay man always runs the risk of identifying with culturally dominant images of misogynist males . . . A more or less secret sympathy with heterosexual male misogyny carries with it the narcissistically gratifying reward of confirming our membership in (and not simply our erotic appetite for) the privileged male society. (p. 64)

This leads to issues raised by Grosz (1995) about the role of the body in her discussion of systematic structures of power in relation to the positioning of gay subjects in response to homophobia and sexual oppression. In arguing that "relations of domination and subordination constituting oppression are more complicated than the occupation of fixed, stable positions of power and powerlessness or centrality and marginality," she raises the question of intrahierarchical power relationships among lesbians and gay men:

> [Are there] specific modalities of oppression experienced by women in general, by lesbians and gay men, by various perverts, transsexuals, transvestites, drag queens, butches, cross-dressers, and all over variations of sexual transgression? This is the anti-humanist question: do the apparently universal characteris-

tics common to all modes of oppression include all types of oppression? If they do, then in what ways do they help to explain
misogyny and homophobia in their specificity? If they only
serve to characterise oppression but not to specify its homophobic dimension, then what needs to be added to them or modified
in them to make them appropriate? These questions give rise to
a series of further anxieties: Is there such a thing as homophobia, and a common oppression for both lesbian and gays? Do
lesbians experience the same forms of homophobia as gay men?
Can we presume that it takes on universal forms? (p. 211)

Given the previous responses and many gay men's active appropriation of straight-acting masculinities, which are conceived as iterative practices of gender subjectification, the body does matter in
terms of the specific forms of homophobia that are experienced by
gay men as a result of being positioned as effeminate and thus a
feminized faggot or queen. How this applies to butch lesbians in their
visibility within a culture that uses the gendered body as a site of
panopticonic surveillance for marking out sexual deviance and differentiation also requires further analysis in light of the questions posed
by Grosz. The gendered body becomes the site for revealing the truth
about our sexuality, and this is effected through the policing of the
boundaries of a naturalized and "normal" heterosexuality read through
the lens of embodied signifying and performative practices of gendered
subjectification (see also Steinberg, Epstein, & Johnson, 1997).

FRAMING THE SEXUAL SUBJECT

Straightacting.com As a Site for Reinscribing Hierarchical Masculinities

The cultural constraints under which we operate include not
only visible political structures but also the fantasmatic processes by which we eroticise the real. Even if we are straight or
gay at birth, we still have to learn to desire particular men and
women, and not to desire others; the economy of our sexual desires is a cultural achievement. (Bersani, 1995:64)

The introduction to the straightacting.com Web site draws further attention to the problematic of normalization in gay men's lives and how it is disguised or rationalized through the invocation of the voluntarist subject who merely prefers or desires a certain kind of man. As Butler argues:

> (a) gender performativity cannot be theorized apart from the forcible and reiterative practice of regulatory sexual regimes; (b) the account of agency conditioned by those norms cannot be conflated with voluntarism or individualism, much less with consumerism, and in no way presupposes a choosing subject . . . (Butler, 1993:15)

It is in this sense that claims to being a "regular," "normal" guy who just prefers other "regular," "normal" guys is born out of a naive and liberal humanist sense of individualism and voluntarism. What is erased is knowledge about the regulatory norms that govern such identificatory process which are implicated in these kinds of masculinity-confirming practices: ". . . the materialization of norms requires those identificatory processes by which norms are assumed or appropriated, and these identifications precede and enable the formation of a subject, but are not strictly speaking, performed by the subject" (Butler, 1993: 15). The straightacting.com Web site invokes a voluntarist subject in its naive assertion that the articulation of sexual desire for straight-acting gay men constitutes what amounts to an instance of the gay male subject exercising his free will or choice:

> Chances are that if you're gay, a minority, or both, you've dealt with some form of discrimination in the past. Unlike what other people might say, calling someone "straight acting" or someone looking for someone else that is "straight acting" is not a way to "diminish gays as human beings or marginalize the gay community." It's called *preference* . . . nothing more, nothing less. *Don't discriminate against people that express their preference!*
>
> Just as people have preferences for the type of guys they like, for example, "Tall men," many of us have a preference for "straight acting" men—men that have very few effeminate traits but still like to get down with other men. ("About Us," straightacting.com Web site)

The very definition of "straight-acting masculinity" as an embodied performative practice materializes here through differentiation from

the feminized and abjected Other. It is in this sense that sexual preference is governed by quite specific gender norms that are erased
through the invocation of a voluntarist subject who merely prefers a
certain sort of guy. At the basis of such assertions or accounts are certain identificatory and signifying processes through which the body
materializes and which cannot be taken for granted or reduced to a
question of mere preference for a certain sort of sexed body. In short,
"identificatory processes are already implicated in a symbolic order
through which the materiality of language and that of the world [or
body] it seeks to signify are perpetually negotiated" (Butler, 1993:
69). However, with regard to the identificatory practices surrounding
the performativity of straight-acting gay masculinities, there appears
to be some foreclosure in the accounts that are offered of the materiality of embodied masculinity which erase the "social and political
locatedness" of the body in its physicality. However, what is significant, as Butler's work exemplifies, are the meanings that are attached
to the body, how it is signified by gay men as a potentially eroticized
site for displacing the abjected feminized other (see also Bersani,
1995). The norms governing the materialized body for many gay men
are signaled through the deployment of the discursive category "straight-
acting" that is propelled and structured according to the imperative to
dispel the abjected and feminized Other. In this sense, for these gay
men, "the process of signification is always material" in terms of how
masculinities get embodied, the underside of which are those "relations of differentiation that tacitly structure and propel signification"
(Butler, 1993:68).

However, it is important to stress that not all gay men support the
norms that propel the signification of straight-acting masculinities
and the misogynist system of repudiating the feminized Other. The
discussion about the fear and avoidance of effeminate gay men was
initiated by the following gay man who posted this note on a
straightacting.com discussion board:

> Always noticed that whoever you talk to there will always be a cer-
> tain percentage of gays who go on about effeminate men—like, "If I
> wanted an effeminate man I may as well go for the real thing . . . a
> woman." "Why do they have to act like a fairy?"—you get the pic-
> ture. Some think it will ruin their reputation to be seen with an ef-
> feminate man. But in my mind I suspect that there may be a little
> homophobia or at least double standards going on in all of this be-
> cause we are asking straight society to accept us for what we are

yet many of us have little toleration for effeminate gay guys. Homo-phobia, double standards? Who agrees or disagrees? Are you un-comfortable or even hostile around effeminate men?

What follows is a selection of responses by gay men who interrogate the limiting and constraining effects imposed by the label "straight-acting":

> I think it's something ya find in every societial sub-group. There's al-ways some who finds fault with the mannerisms and behavior of their own. Either they feel these "others" are perpetuatin' the ste-reotype or affectin' behavior to "fit in" with the larger society. There was a time when blacks who spoke well, worked hard, and studied hard to get a degree were called *Uncle Toms* and accused of actin' white. There was a similar period in the Latino/Hispanic groups. I assume the Asian community had/has a similar experience. Maybe it's that I'm an ole dawg—but I don't really care too much 'bout a person's behavior or mannerisms so long as they're genuine and reasonably venue appropriate . . . Orientation is irrelevant . . . Per-haps it's the fear of the stigma and bein' less than comfortable in their own skins that causes folks to react that way toward their own.

> Your masculinity, and your personality is rested in your concept of maleness: how men behave and what they do. These guys just have a different concept, a different way of being themselves than you do. I don't think of them as women, I think of them as men who have a different take on it. Honestly, we're all men, we've all got our quirks and personality traits that make us who we are. We can't all be the Marlboro man, nor should we try to be. How dull life would be if we were all the same way.

> Not trying to be PC here, but when folks say "I want a real man" or "a man who acts like a man, not a woman," it's very ambiguous and a little insulting. Our notions of gender and gender traits are con-stantly evolving. Most of the guys on this board wouldn't be caught dead in a wig and tights—but that's exactly what *real* men wore a couple hundred years ago.

Such responses indicate the potential for a politics of disruption com-mitted to interrogating dominant notions of masculinity in gay men's lives as signified by the appropriation of the category "straight-act-ing" which is founded on the power of discourse to circumscribe though not limit a particular domain of intelligibility regarding the constitution of masculinities in gay men's lives. This notion of a politics and ethics of male sexual practices and gendered subjectification is taken up in greater detail in the following section.

TOWARD A POLITICS AND ETHICS OF MALE SEXUAL PRACTICE AND RELATEDNESS

> Our fantasy investments are often countered by more consciously and more rationally elaborated modes of reaching out to others. Such as liking or admiring people we don't desire. In that tension lies an important moral dimension of our political engagement. (Bersani, 1995:64)

It is important to remember that while Web sites such as straightacting. com and gay chat rooms such as gay.com are sites for the reappropriation and eroticization of particular forms of masculinity fortified in the dominant culture, there are gay men using these sites who interrogate the norms governing the gendered subjectification of the sexed body. The subversive potential is always present in the impossibility of ever fully inhabiting straight-acting masculinity as a specific identificatory and performative practice through which many gay men's subject formation is mobilized (see Butler, 1993).

> If a performative provisionally succeeds (and I will suggest that "success" is always and only provisional), then it is not because an intention successfully governs the action of speech, but only because that action echoes prior actions, and accumulates the force of authority through repetition or citation of a prior authoritative set of practices. (Butler, 1993:227)

Thus, the citational and performative practice of straight-acting masculinity is not authorized by the intentions of the gay male subject, but is mobilized through historically specific sets of power relations. Butler rejects a political interventionist queer agenda that involves recourse to a self-determining and self-naming sexual subject through the assertion of identity categories. In short, she argues for a queer interventionist politics and activism that rejects invoking the ahistorical, self-determining, and naming subject through the realization of a specific queer or LGBT subjectivity (1993).

Although the appropriation of straight-acting masculinities by many gays is often understood in terms of the totalizing self-determining subject who is merely expressing a choice or a preference, it is important to emphasize that this is only a temporary form of totalization compelled by certain social imperatives and modes of citationality.

According to Butler, there is always the promise of deregulation of the gender norms that require the embodiment of certain idealized forms of masculinity and femininity which are underscored, she argues, by "the idealization of the heterosexual bond" (1993:232). The idealization of masculinity, symbolized by the discursive invocation of the category of straight-acting, compels a certain corporeally enacted masculinity, but it can never fully approximate the ideal form which is always already haunted by the specter of the repudiated and feminized Other. It is in this sense that straight-acting masculinity is not determined by the gay male subject but is the result of "the forcible citation of a norm" that is needed in order to qualify as and to remain a viable or acceptably masculine subject (Butler, 1993:232).

Embedded in such acts of subjectification for gay men are complex and historically specific power relations of regulation and punishment that have been reinforced through the apparatus of the law and religion, as well as through disciplinary regimens and practices of medicine and psychiatry, all of which have inscribed the gay male sexual subject as deviant and perverse (see Foucault, 1977, 1978). As I have illustrated, the effects of such discourses drive and underscore many gay men's psychic and corporeal investment in straight-acting masculinities. This calls for attention to the possibilities for interrogating the norms that govern and compel the authorization and legitimation of becoming a viable masculine and sexual subject. This must necessarily involve challenging the normalizing tendency to construct and constitute gay men or queer male subjects as particular kinds of gendered subjects. It must also involve some interrogation of the ethics of a particular male sexual identity that is founded on sexual oppression and internalization of hierarchical gender regimes (Kendall, 1999; Stoltenberg, 1989).

Warner (1999), however, in arguing for an interrogation of the ethics of sexual shame, advocates "a program of change [that] should be accountable to the queer ethos [and] responsible to the lived arrangements of queer life, and articulated in queer publics" (p. 146). He advocates "an accessible sexual culture," one that embraces "the gay male practice of public sex" and in so doing rejects the taboo of public sex as a challenge to the legitimation and privatization of sex in marriage (p. 177). According to Warner, the queer ethos must negate constructing and treating gay men "simply as a mass of deviants looking for hormonally driven release" (p. 177). In this sense, he argues for the need to challenge representations of gay men "as over-sexed monsters of the urban alleys and the highway rest-room" (p. 181) and to resignify public sex as a form of "eroticize[d] participation in the public world of their privacy" (p. 179). He also rejects the anti-porn activism and rhetoric, which perpetuates a discourse of "sleaze," "filth," and "smut" (p. 181) and claims that "what is traded in pornographic commerce is not just speech, privately consumed; it is publicly certifiable recognition."

Dowsett (1996) also advocates "the enactment of sex" as constitutive of men's sexual subjectivity referring to "the collective pursuit of sensation and pleasure, in/with youth, with oneself and two/three/more others" as "a public disavowal of private sex":

> There is no need to redeem sex as pluralist polymorphous pleasure, opening the way for the transformation of anti-sexual societies—nice as that might be. Its recognized collective enactment, and even the inciting possibility of it, offer possibilities far more wicked and wilful. Its capacity to transform relations between men . . . Any man who has taken another man's cock up his arse knows only too well that sex will never be the same again. Any man who has done so "twenty to thirty times in a night" knows something about men's sexual capacities that cannot be snuffed out by HIV/AIDS or anything else. The transformation in desire produced by gay communities, this collective reinscription of transgressive desire, best signified by the rapacious desiring anus, will endure beyond the epidemic. (Dowsett, 1996:212-213)

What is not addressed in advocating the subversive and supposedly transformative practices of gay male sex is some interrogation of the norms that compel the appropriation and perpetuation of certain hierarchical power relations among gay men (see Bergling, 2001; Alvear, 2003; Lambert, Chapter 6 in this collection). Moreover, Dowsett argues that gay men symbolically divest themselves of their power as men, but in their very avid pursuit of these mutual pleasures, in their multiple encounters, they refuse to enact power in sex by "re-presenting the internalized phallic male as infinitely loved object of sacrifice" (1996:209). Mutual or reciprocal sexual practice is constituted as democratic and outside the ambit of a phallic symbolic order that is invested in traditional male power. Moreover, for Dowsett, pornography is constituted as a site for enabling the equalization of power through sexual relations between men. He argues that the industry "specializes in fantasy" and presents sex as a performance where men are constituted as sexually active whether they are engaging in receptive or penetrative sex acts. It is in this sense, Dowsett claims, that they "embody desire in action":

> What the anti-porn crusaders seem to forget is that the penis cannot subjugate by definition where there are two penises present and where pleasure is allocated evenly between the men— they both come, something that cannot be faked by male porn stars—and dispersed among penises, anuses, and other body parts. In gay porn then, the narrative is discursively informed by, as it is formative of, the designation of anal intercourse between men as democratic and immensely mutually pleasurable. (Dowsett, 1996:206-207)

What is denied in such an analysis of supposedly transgressive sexual practices between gay men is an analysis of certain forms of male power that are supposedly disavowed through engaging in mutually pleasurable and reciprocal sexual activities. The reality of many gay men's complicity in sexual oppression and thus in certain power relations which confer a viable idealized masculinity is not addressed in what amounts to an idealization of transgression as it is enacted by gay men through the sorts of sexual practices that they engage in. His point that "the penis cannot subjugate when there are two penises present" ignores the broader social systems of power through which desire is enacted and shaped. What is not emphasized are the hierarchical power relationships that get played out among gay men and the role of gender and sexual oppression in their lives (see Bergling, 2001; Alvear, 2003; Burfitt, 1998). In this sense, the articulation of "queer" or "homo" sex and politics must be understood as discursively constituted according to the dictates of a specific grid of intelligibility and regulatory schema for representing gay men as particular kinds of sexual and gendered subjects.

The norms governing the anxiety-provoking discourses surrounding the gay male body as a potential site for the reinscription and reidealization of hegemonic power relations are erased in the constitution of their sexual practices as a site for sexual liberation and freedom. For both Warner and Dowsett, an interrogation of the particular roles that pornography and gay chat rooms have the potential to play in emphasizing certain normative "stats" within a regulatory schema that dictates penis size ("well hung") and body performativity (gym-toned, no body hair, and straight-acting) are excluded from a discourse that celebrates and idealizes gay male sexuality.

THE LIMITS OF SEXUAL LIBERATION

The work of Alvear (2003) is an excellent source for exposing the limits of such a queer form of sexual politics and ethics of queer life (see also Bergling, 2001). He documents the anxieties, concerns, and worries that gay men have about sex and portrays a very different reality to that offered by Warner and Dowsett. In his book *Men Are Pigs, But We Love Bacon* (2003), which includes a range of gay men writing to seek advice from Alvear, as one of "America's most outrageous sex columnists," he provides insight into the lived realities of gay men's relations and perceptions. He documents, for example, the intensification of fear about penis size in gay men's sex lives, which he claims "draws most of the letters" (2003:5). He uses humor and often sardonic wit to deflate the myths about penis size and provides statistics from condom manufacturers who report that "only 6 percent of the male population needs extra large condoms" (p. 5). His tactic is to interrupt and disrupt the norms that compel a form of gay male subjectivity that invests in a reidealization of the body. Through the confessional space that is constituted we are provided with narratives that foreground the particular role that self-monitoring and surveillance play in many gay men's lives. Such policing is dictated by the often normative and normalizing gaze of other gay males who are hierarchically positioned within regulatory schemas for framing the male body and the gay male sexual subject. By also including letters written in response to gay men who find themselves in desperate or troubled circumstances, what emerges is a potentially transgressive interventionist politics organized, not so much around a norm that compels an idealization of gay male sexuality, but rather one that highlights the potential for gay men to embrace a particular ethic of empathic relatedness and compassion for other gay men built on a rejection of depersonalization. A particular example is given through the response of a gay man who writes about his quite small "flaccid dick," which has resulted in many gay men dismissing him once he is naked. He documents the abusive responses he has received, such as "Your dick is so tiny, it could fit through the top of a coke bottle" (p. 45). He also reveals that honest friends have confessed their inability to continue a sexual relationship with him due to the small size of his penis. One close friend, to whom he was sexually attracted, but had never been sexually intimate, also confessed that he had heard from a former boyfriend about his penis size. This resulted, the letter writer claims, in the assertion that he could only "get aroused by big dicks" and, therefore, could not consider having a sexual relationship with him.

This incident in itself highlights the role of surveillance at the hands of other gay men who are differentially positioned in terms of appropriating regulatory power that enables them to crudely reduce and depersonalize another gay man on the basis of his penis size. The effects of the norms compelling such objectifying and depersonalizing practices need to be named and called in the manner articulated by Alvear, who, in response to this letter, claims:

> You think straight society is judgemental and hostile? Welcome to the loving and accepting brotherhood of gay men. Your letter perfectly captured the cruelty and emotional brutality gay men struggle against in their own community. (2003:47)

He also constructs such practices as severely limiting the range of sexual options available to gay men. He presents such behavior as constituting an act of shaming that is embedded in power relationships that relate to straight society's enforced inferiorization of gay men, who themselves, in turn, accrue a sense of power by putting other gay men down. However, the inclusion and force of other gay men's responses to this letter are powerful in highlighting their sense of compassion, as well as their capacities for embracing alternative norms that enable the materialization of a desire that is less restrictive and limiting:

> I love sweet, tender, compassionate men . . . dick size means almost nothing. I wish that guy were here right now . . . I would love to send him a note. (p. 48)

> After reading that letter by "Not that small," I felt so bad for him I wanted to cry. Please tell him that not every one is a size queen. (pp. 48-49)

> Although I *love* being a gay man, I hate shallow, condescending, and just plain mean-spirited our community can be sometimes. I hope this guy realizes that not all gay men are like this . . . (p. 49)

Alvear also includes letters by gay men who buy into "all the ugly stereotypes of receptive anal sex" in constructing "bottoms" as sissies and who believe that "getting fucked by someone less masculine makes you less masculine" (p. 197). His response once again constitutes a form of interventionist politics committed to interrogating the depersonalizing effects of labels and the deployment of a particular form of heterosexualized male power:

> The only thing gay men seem to like more than assuming the position is assuming an identity. Oddly we've created whole identities out of sexual positions . . . Sex has a glorious unlimited horizon. It's unchartered territory no matter how many times we've been there before . . . And the best description we can come up with is "top" and "bottom"? We suck. Labels take you from liberty to limitation in sixty self-adhesive seconds. If you perform a sexually aggressive act, labels demand you take on a sexually aggressive persona. If you perform a sexually receptive act, labels mandate the conception of submissive identity. Label-love turns the principles of pleasure into the politics of penetration. (pp. 186-187)

In this sense, Alvear draws attention to the meanings that gay men attach to certain sex acts within a regulatory schema that reduces sexuality to a binary classificatory system of gender signification that is maintained by the apparatus of heterosexuality. What is opened up by Alvear are discursive spaces and practices for naming, interrogating, and disputing certain norms that have very real effects and consequences for gay men's emotional, physical, and sexual well-being.

Moreover, he foregrounds the kinds of oppressive and depersonalizing effects of certain power relations implicated in the articulation of desire and pleasure for many gay men. Thus, a politics committed to encouraging some critical interrogation of the power relations driving gay men's "fantasy investments" and "erotic interests" and the tensions between these and other modes of relatedness that involve reaching out to other gay men whom they do not necessarily desire (Bersani, 1995) constitutes an interface of potentially disruptive politics in its capacity to subvert the "regimes of the normal" in gay men's lives, particularly in relation to destabilizing the regulatory constraints of a structure of eroticized, phallic male supremacy (Stoltenberg, 1989).

As Bersani (1995) argues, the focus needs to be on interrogating normalizing regimes of practice that imprison "the eroticised body within a rigidly gendered sexuality, in which pleasure is at once recognized and legitimized as a function of genital differences between the sexes" (p. 4). This has been illustrated in this chapter in relation to examining the tendency of many gay men to invest in and eroticize straight-acting masculinities which have assimilative consequences in terms of mobilizing the gendered and sexual hierarchies sustained by the apparatus of heterosexuality. Hence, what is needed is a sexual politics and an ethics of male sexual practice and relatedness that can "free us from an oppressive psychology of desire as lack," from an oppressive sexual regime and normalizing practice that compels a misogynist repudiation of the feminized Other (Bersani, 1995:7).

In fact, Bersani argues that increased visibility of gay men and lesbian women, rather than contributing to sexual liberation, historically has led to further intensification of homophobic regimes of surveillance:

> . . . visibility is a precondition of surveillance, disciplinary intervention, and, at the limit, gender cleansing. The classification into character types of how people imagine and pursue their bodies' pleasures greatly reduced the heterogeneity of erotic behavior. (Bersani, 1995:11)

This "gender cleansing" continues to resurface, perhaps even more vigorously than ever before, through the deployment and appropriation of the identificatory label of "straight-acting masculinity" as a regulatory system for inscribing the sexed body. In fact, according to

Bersani, "just about everything we take for granted about sexuality and sex, even the very differences between the sexes, may be to a significant degree learned, and that to unlearn it all may be our greatest political challenge" (p. 35). Thus he advocates a particular politics organized around interrogating "modalities of desire [as not] only effects of social operations," but as being at the heart of how "erotic desire for the same might revolutionize our understanding of how the human subject is, or might be, socially implicated" (p. 73). This means drawing attention to the norms governing the social structures and relations of power through which gay men come to understand themselves as particular kinds of embodied, gendered, and sexual subjects. It must necessarily involve an interrogation of the "connection between the way we take our pleasure and the way we exercise power" (Bersani, 1995:80).

This imbrication of our pleasures within broader forms of social organization is exemplified by Bersani in his analysis of S/M as a site for the inscription of society's oppressive power structures through which conventional masculinity gets legitimated. He adds that it is not so much the "networks of power and authority" that get challenged as gay men's exclusion from these networks (p. 85). This practice on one level then functions as a compensatory mechanism for accruing and experiencing a form of power that is often denied to gay men in the dominant culture:

> Most significantly, at least in gay male S/M leather scene, conventional masculinity is worshipped. While the oxymoronic phenomenon of the leather queen is often seen as attacking straight ideas of extreme masculinity, it actually expands the notion of machismo. (Bersani, 1995:85)

Thus S/M is often understood as an attempt on behalf of gay men to reclaim a masculinity that has been denied to them. It is about breaking the stereotypic casting of gay men as effeminate. However, Bersani appears to be calling into question the liberatory or emancipatory potential of such practices. Once again it is the displacement of the ever-haunting specter of the feminized faggot that is at the core of such a rationalization and which leads to reinstating rather than subverting or transforming hegemonic social practices of masculine domination. According to Bersani, some advocates claim that there is a sense of a game being played in S/M through which the reversibility of master/slave roles is read as constituting a subversive performative practice that poses a challenge to the very social hierarchies of power. What is acknowledged and recognized, Bersani argues, is the excitement and pleasure derived from engaging in such power relations, but which clearly amount to a reiteration of a norm that dictates the imagination of pleasure determined and framed in terms articulated by the dominant culture. In this sense, he considers S/M to be a deeply conservative practice in terms of its imagination of pleasure, which is dictated by specific norms for inscribing hegemonic masculinity (1995: 87-88).

It is in this sense that playing out or enactment of power as a strategic game within erotic relationships, while not reproducing the intentionality supporting oppressive power structures of domination in the broader culture, still supports the norms that govern such power structures for "[w]hat is the game without the power structure that constitutes its strategies?" (Bersani, 1995:88). It is in this sense that "S/M shares the dominant culture's obsession with power, it simply asks that culture to consider exercising power in contexts where roles are not fixed . . ." (p. 91):

> S/M, far from dissociating itself from a fascistic master-slave relation, actually confirms an identity between that relation and its own practices. It removes masters and slaves from economic and racial superstructures, thus confirming the eroticism of the master-slave configuration. (p. 89)

What is emphasized once again is the allure of hegemonic masculine power in terms of how it gets taken on by some gay men and eroticized. In fact, it is its eroticized potential that is repressed within oppressive social structures of domination in the straight world. The subversive potential of S/M is derived not so much from the playing out of a particular power game which emulates structures of domination and submission found in the dominant culture, but from a reading of S/M that foregrounds the reiterative effects of the very norms that reproduce a system of masculine power that gets taken on and eroticized by gay men.

Such readings do raise questions about the potential of what Butler (1993) terms the "hyperbolic gesture" of the performative dimensions of excessive sexuality of which S/M may be considered an example. The norms that compel the investment of gay men in forms of masculinity and eroticized power that are mobilized and reiterated through engaging in S/M are invested in reclamation of hegemonic masculine power whose damaging effects have been discussed in this chapter in its focus on the appropriation and corporeal significance of the category of "straight-acting" and its signifying potential in gay men's lives, given the reiteration of norms that compel investing in hegemonic structures of eroticized masculinity.

CONCLUSION

The focus in this chapter, on one level, has been on the policing of masculinities and the sexed body as a site for eroticized identificatory practices. I have attempted to illustrate how such practices for many gay men are imbued in certain social relations and gender hierarchies that limit and constrain the potentiality for addressing the machinations and dynamics of power and shaming in their lives (see Alvear, 2003). Straight-acting masculinities, hence, emerge in this chapter as a pivotal focus for examining the identificatory processes and practices by which a significant number of gay men come to understand themselves as particular kinds of gendered and sexual subjects. What has been highlighted is the extent to which straight-acting signifies the intensification of regulatory norms that propel "a desire for the same" and an erotic interest that is always haunted by the specter of the denigrated and repudiated Other epitomized by the feminized faggot or queen. Within a sociocultural context in which specific discourses about straight-acting masculinities gain a particular authoritative status or ascendancy—for example, from "Bears" who claim that they don't engage in "faggoty sex" to "gainers" who deliberately put on weight to adopt a particular way of being masculine that challenges the idealization of the gay male body (Naod, 2003)—I have been concerned in this chapter to draw attention to the regulatory and constraining effects of certain norms and imperatives governing the identificatory processes and labels that many gay men take up in these performative and self-fashioning practices of corporeal gendered subjectification (Butler, 1993). The way forward is to move beyond a queer political agenda that prioritizes a particular ethics that is organized around an idealization of gay men's sexual practices as a site for transformative and subversive possibilities to one which is committed to interrogating sexual oppression and hierarchies in gay men's lives and their complicity in a sex-gender system built on a form of misogyny, internalized homophobia, and a reclamation of hegemonic masculinity.

REFERENCES

Alvear, M. (2003). *Men are pigs, but we love bacon.* New York: Kensington Books.

Bergling, T. (2001). *Sissyphobia: Gay men and effeminate behavior.* Binghamton, NY: Harrington Park Press.

Bersani, L. (1995). *Homos.* Cambridge, MA: Harvard University Press.

Burfitt, J. (1998). Straight Acting? *Outrage,* 187:36-38.

Butler, J. (1993). *Bodies that matter: On the discursive limits of sex.* London: Routledge.

Coleman, W. (1990). Doing masculinity/doing theory. In J. Hearn & D. Morgan (Eds.), *Men, masculinities and social theory* (p. 186-203) London: Unwin Hyman.

Connell, B. (1995). *Masculinities.* Sydney: Allen & Unwin.

Connell, R. W. (1992). A very straight gay: Masculinity, homosexual experience, and the dynamics of gender, *American Sociological Review, 57:*735-751.

Connell, R.W. (2002). *Gender.* Cambridge, UK: Polity.

Dowsett, G. (1996). *Practising desire: Homosexual sex in the era of AIDS.* Stanford, CA: Stanford University Press.

Foucault, M. (1977). *Discipline and punish.* London: Penguin.

Foucault, M. (1978). *The history of sexuality,* Volume 1. Trans. R. Hurley. New York: Vintage.

Foucault, M. (1984). Preface to *The history of sexuality,* Volume 2. In P. Rabinow (Ed.), *The Foucault reader* (pp. 333-339). London: Penguin.

Foucault, M. (1985). *The history of sexuality,* Volume 2. Trans. R. Hurley. New York: Vintage.

Foucault, M. (1986). *The history of sexuality,* Volume 3. Trans. R. Hurley. New York: Vintage.

Fuss, D. (1991). *Inside/Out: Lesbian theories, gay theories.* New York & London: Routeledge.

Grosz, E. (1995). *Space, time and perversion.* Sydney: Allen & Unwin.

Harding, J. (1998). *Sex acts: Practices of femininity and masculinity.* London: Sage.

Hutton, P. (1988). Foucault, Freud, and the technologies of the self. In L. Martin, H. Gutman, and P. Hutton (Eds.), *Technologies of the self* (pp. 121-144). Amherst: The University of Massachusetts Press.

Kaufman, M. (1999). Men, feminism and men's contradictory experiences of power. In J.A. Kuypers (Ed.), *Men and power* (pp. 75-103). New York: Prometheus Books.

Kendall, C. (1999). Gay male pornography/gay male community: Power without consent, mimicry without subversion. In J.A. Kuypers (Ed.), *Men and power* (pp. 195-213). New York: Prometheus Books.

Kimmel, M. (1999). Masculinity as homophobia: Fear, shame and silence in the construction of gender identity. In J.A. Kuypers (Ed.), *Men and power* (pp. 105-128). New York: Prometheus Books.

Martino, W. (2000). Policing masculinities: Investigating the role of homophobia and heteronormativity in the lives of adolescent boys at school. *The Journal of Men's Studies,* 8(2):213-236.

Martino, W. & Pallotta-Chiarolli, M. (2003). *So what's a boy? Addressing issues of masculinity and schooling.* Philadelphia: Open University Press.

Messner, M. (1997). *Politics of masculinities: Men in movements.* Thousand Oaks, CA: Sage.

Naod, S. (2003). Totally phat!, *DNA Magazine,* 43:46-47.

Renold, E. (2003). "If you don't kiss me, you're dumped": Boys, boyfriends and heterosexualised masculinities in the primary school. *Education Review,* 55(2): 179-194.

Rose, N. (1989). *Governing the soul: The shaping of the private self.* London: Routledge.

Steinberg, D. L., Epstein, D., & Johnson, R. (1997). *Border patrols: Policing the boundaries of heterosexuality.* London: Cassell.

Stoltenberg, J. (1989). *Refusing to be a man: Essays on sex and justice.* New York: Meridian.

Stoltenberg, J. (1999). How power makes men: The grammar of gender identity. In J.A. Kuypers (Ed.), *Men and power* (pp. 35-51). New York: Prometheus Books.

Warner, M. (1999). *The trouble with normal: Sex politics, and the ethics of queer life.* New York: The Free Press.

Chapter 6

Stats Please: Gay Men As Mimics, Robots, and Commodities in Contemporary Cultural Spaces

Anthony Lambert

... gay is to straight *not* as copy is to original, but rather as copy is to copy. The parodic repetition of "the original" ... reveals the original to be nothing other than a parody of the *idea* of the natural and the original. (Butler, 1990:31)

Publicly performed "gay male" behavior is organized, promoted, and underwritten by specific terms of participation—its relationship to an *idea* of the "straight" masculine. This chapter explores a range of physical and virtual spaces within which gay men represent themselves to others and within which they are constructed generally. I am interested in the ways in which gay men perform particularized and contextual versions of masculinity, in short how they perform "the copy" (in Butler's, 1990, sense) of both "maleness" and "gayness" through mimicry and redefinition. From Internet environments to reality TV, certain forms of self-fashioning and textual representation reveal not only copies of a "parodic idea" of a masculine "original," but also an exclusive, limited ordering and commodification of gay male bodies and desires.

A need exists to interrogate the circumstances in which gay men are allowed to "act" in given environments. Performing the "idealized masculine" is their ticket to participation in a series of (gay and straight) spaces and activities. Playing the robotic, numerically ordered "man," with big muscles, a big dick, and a tough outlook is an easy way of forestalling the misogynistic fear and consternation surrounding the "feminine" in gay men. Hypermasculine excess and

mimicry of the mythic "straight man" within constructions of gayness often imply that there is a "right" way to be gay. Yet the fact that
"straight-acting" is any kind of acting at all reveals the copying of
masculinity to be another kind of drag, affecting the possible social
and textual outcomes for both heterosexual and homosexual men in a
range of given spaces.

Publicly, gay men can perform identities outside of this "copy"
only when the containable aspects of their "queerness" can be seen to
hold some usefulness within heteronormative contexts. Queerness
and effeminacy are acceptable when they are deemed to be positively
contributing to a straight world, repackaged as effective commodities
emptied of their politics, which can entertain mainstream audiences
and teach a lesson or two about hygiene and style without rocking the
boat. As Susan Faludi (1999:42) has argued, "gay culture, as it gets
increasingly absorbed into the larger commercial culture, becomes
increasingly muted in its challenge of masculine roles."

The purposeful problematizing of recent representations brings us
closer to understanding how normalizing practices produce gay men,
physically and psychically, as gendered outcasts: homosexual males
whose environmental assimilation is made possible only through the
enactment of a vocabulary that reduces both the visibility and value
of difference. From the hypermasculine to the queer we will see how
the acceptable performance of gay male identities in contemporary
cultural spaces has an explicit relationship to numbers and currency
in the processes of both copying and constructing the masculine—
how the statistical perfection and "value" of the masculine body and
commercial viability of queerness both contribute to the "parodic repetition" of supposedly natural and original forms of maleness.

VIRTUALLY GAY MEN, OR GAY BY NUMBERS

Homosexual communities have always sought to create or find
spheres of activity in which both the "freedom of expression" and
"safety" lacking in the dominant heteronormative structuring of social spaces can be found. Certainly virtual environments can be seen
to promote the idea of such freedom and the possibility of identity
and activity without limits. Mirzoeff (1999:107) states that "in the
early years of their existence, the Internet and other virtual environments also seemed to offer new forms of sexual and gender identity."

There is a distinct tension, however, between possibility and practice. Mirzoeff (1999:107) explains that "in principle virtual environments are race and gender blind to the extent that these critical markers of identity in everyday life might become superfluous in cyberspace. While this utopian possibility is still available in theory, the results so far have not been encouraging."

This in itself is not entirely surprising. Yet like any realm of human interaction, the Internet is a space within which the notion of community is able to function effectively only through the creating and sustaining of conjuncturally specific sets of protocols. The title of this investigation, "stats please," is taken from one such protocol through which gay men greet one another in online chat rooms. Standard introductory lines such as "hey"" or "are you busy?" still exist within the chat space of Web sites such as gay.com, but only as a prelude to a descriptive exchange of measurements, physical attributes, and sexual tastes. For the uninitiated gay male (or newly virtual gay male), frequent users of such spaces are more than willing to educate fledgling cyber-gays (in my own experience, and no doubt that of other users) by explaining that stats is short for statistics. Although photographs are now routinely attached to profiles, the information required under the rubric of stats may include hair color, eye color, and race, but is more often connected to age, height, weight, and, most important, penis size ("cut" or "uncut" is also an important specific which one may be asked to clarify if it is not stated in the first response). Identities and bodies are summarized, sanitized, and modified to fit an immediate communal and environmental purpose. Rather than promoting difference in a political or individualistic sense, they are reduced to an easily reproduced code of manliness, the definition of what gay men should desire *to have* and desire *to be*.

The "stats please" virtual protocol may be seen as a tidy and effective way of reducing the amount of time wasted on the computer seeking out an appropriate sex partner. It may even be viewed in rather simplistic terms as a crude kind of language, which enables "smoother" and more direct communications between gay men within virtual space. At the same time, these observations cannot remain separate from the idea that "lesbian and gay communities exist as discursive phenomena" and that "their status as virtual and textual does not make them any less real" (McKee, 1997:24). Barker's (2000:20) understanding of Foucauldian discourse as referring "to the regulated production of knowledge through language which gives meaning to both material objects and social practices" reminds one that the "stats please" greeting has a lot more to it than a "hi, I just wanna get an idea of what you look like" quality (made especially obvious where photos are already included in profiles). It is simultaneously a command, a marker for identity, an explicit judgment, and a call to mimicry of the "str8forward," "str8-acting" approach to "man-on-man" action. Indeed, and perhaps most important, it is an initiation and a guarantee of the rules; it is another form of learning from other gay men, behaviorally and subjectively, how to be a "gay male" in *this space*. The problematic discursive construction of "value" and "currency" in these limited terms is foregrounded, and the reduction of individual difference can thus be tied to a set of governing norms, which attempt to write an undifferentiated version of the sexualized gay male body.

OF MIMICRY AND HETEROTOPIC SPACEMEN

So the "stats please" command/greeting is not simply a case of "when in Rome . . ." It is an entry into language and subjectivity, a discourse of the "masculine" attached to a particular environment and enacted through the mimicry of existing norms (surrounding Butler's "parodic ideal" of some originary form of maleness). The workings of this process can be illuminated to some extent through the observations of French phenomenologist Roger Caillois (1984), who identifies an overlapping between physical mimicry in the insect world and the psychological insecurity of human beings as they attempt to bridge the gap between personality and environment. The tendency to mimic represents (using Grosz's, 1995, interpretation of Caillois) "a correlate of one's ability to locate oneself as the point of origin or reference of space" (p. 90). Mimicry in Caillois's (1984:30) sense is a process of "depersonalisation by assimilation to space." The human being's need to mimic existing languages and behaviors mirrors in many ways the phenomenon of mimicry in the biological world of animals, plants, and insects. Such an observation, to quote Caillois (1984:23), is not so "gratuitous as it sounds" as "there seem to exist in man (sic) the psychological potentialities" which correlate to the conditions of the biological mimetic process.

This process is therefore connected to notions of both identity and "fitting in." In this sense the idea that gay men mimic one another (in virtual, textual, or physically "real" spaces), and certain imagined ideals, facilitates a blurring between self and environment in which they are less likely to stick out (for the *wrong* reasons) and can claim or create an "identity." Grosz (1995:88) states:

> Mimesis is particularly significant in outlining the ways in which the relations between an organism and its environment are blurred and confused—the way in which its environment is not clearly distinct from the organism, but is an active component of its identity.

The assumption of identity markers attached to the protocols of a given space offers an effective means by which users are able not only to function in a foreign or new "space," but to identify with it and belong in it. This notion of functioning, psychologically and physically, is central to the highly sexualized spaces (from the Internet to bars, dance clubs, and sex clubs) of gay men's social worlds. "Stats please" invokes a reduced or modified version of the gay male's (prehomospatial) self.

"We are thus dealing with a luxury, and even a dangerous luxury," writes Caillois (1984:23), as mimicry is "a real temptation by space" (p. 26). In a biological context this is because "one finds many remains of mimetic insects in the stomachs of predators . . . Conversely, some species that are inedible, and would thus have nothing to fear, are also mimetic" (Caillois, 1984:22-23). So if mimicry is a luxury which can invite unnecessary danger (whether it be a reduced form of the self, or physical harm) how might a critical ethics account for it? In terms of our present discussion, why would gay men mimic other gay men in their already established mimicry of an idealized, imagined masculine position? In Caillois's discussion the answer is an instance of "legendary psychasthenia," that is, a state brought on by "a disturbance in the perception of space" (1984:28). Physical/virtual mimicry is attached to a crisis of represented space in which the connections between self and spatial placement, between consciousness and surroundings are "dispossessed of its privilege" (p. 30). Caillois states that the "search for the similar would seem to be a means, if not an intermediate stage. Indeed the end would seem to be assimilation to the surroundings" (1984:27).

Mimicry is then a means of overcoming spatial displacement and demonstrates the way in which ideas of both "self-preservation" and "renunciation" coexist in self-environment relations. Taken into the realm of self-representation, this mimicry becomes particularly useful for the successful participation of gay men in the "mainstream." Reichen and Chip, the "same-sex" winners of the American reality TV competition *The Amazing Race* on CBS, 2003, went to great lengths to ensure they were promoted within the show as "married," and in the final episode Reichen declared that the muscular pair did not want to be seen as "queeny" or "effeminate," but as "strong," "prepared," and "out to win." After they crossed the finish line, they declared that they were Americans who incidentally "just happened to be gay." The threat of difference is obscured in "masculine" bodies and the normalizing rhetoric of "valid" relationships and "natural" male competitiveness, which ensure they cannot be seen as "out of place." In short, this kind of mimicry can be attached to discourses of assimilation of which there are both subtle and obvious examples from adapting one's behavior, to a chat room, or dressing for the "genre" of a gay club, to a "blurring" of the edges of the self found in representations of gay male relationships. In the recent Australian renovation reality series *The Block,** for instance, the gay male couple—who wore matching underpants, had matching crew cuts, worked out together, hit the beach together, and continually had solariums and oxygen treatments side by side—eventually became known less by their individual names than by their preferred nickname: "the boys" (*The Block,* 2003). Adhering to a parodic ideal/copy of both the masculine body and an ultramodern middle-class masculine space, "the boys" created their bodies, relationship, and environment in palatable terms for an Australian television audience, which peaked at 3.114 million viewers (Casey, 2003). Achieving the idealized "gay masculine" involves a mimicry of renovation, assimilation, and high maintenance.

Without reducing social behavior purely to instinct, or solely to psychological or economic "needs" or "gains," being a gay man in a certain space (including the "relationship space," or even the representational reality TV space) can be said to involve elements of self-construction or, at the very least, self-modification. The point then is

---

The Block (shown across Australia on the Nine Network) followed the lives of four couples (three straight) as they each renovated an apartment in the same block in Sydney's Bondi Beach. It became one of the highest-rating shows in Australian television history.

that so called "codes of conduct" or, rather, repeated, imitative sets of acts can be further linked to explicit discourses, which both circulate in and construct the social spaces gay men are seen to collectively inhabit. This "gay/masculine" emphasis on numbers and statistics (and by association the "buddy," the "bloke," and the hard body/penis) is by no means limited to chat rooms and reality TV. A Sydney sex-on-premises venue ran a series of advertisements in community papers in mid-2002 offering free entry to anyone whose penis was ten inches or longer. The only requirement was that you had to present it for measurement at the front door. In the American version of comedy/soap series *Queer As Folk* (2000–), the only effeminate male character, Emmett, agrees to masturbate live on his best friend's Internet site, after a famous porn star pulls out of the engagement. When it is discovered that Emmett has more inches than most men have seen in their lives, he is suddenly the toast of Pittsburgh, signing autographs at the local nightclub, receiving gifts from fans, being pursued by a local multimillionaire, and winning a coveted porn star award.

The "stats please" mind-set must consequently be understood in terms of its connections to power and the ordering of gay male identities and bodies in social spaces. Foucault (1993:168) argues that space "is fundamental in any form of communal life; space is fundamental in any exercise of power." Foucault identifies that there are spaces within spaces and there are sets of power relations within them; they are heterogeneous spaces. In this way, the multiple spaces of gay "maleness" reveal the means through which certain types of male "gayness" are rewarded and exalted. Foucault's (1986:25) spaces, as "heterotopias" juxtapose "in a single real place several spaces" creating either "a space of illusion that exposes every real space . . . as still more illusory," or a space "that is other, another real space . . . not of illusion, but of compensation" (p. 27). Spatial power is then enacted through shifting notions of both the illusory and the compensatory, which in this case can be expressed in terms of their connections to "ideal" masculinities. The problem for Foucault (1980:149) was the exaltation of historical narrative (as an idealized, if not mythical past) over spatial relationships:

> A whole history remains to be written of *spaces—which* would at the same time be the history of *powers* (both of these terms in the plural)—from the great strategies of geopolitics to the little tactics of habitat.

This would be an ambitious project to say the least. To narrow the focus then, we might see that the numerical value, which frames the shape and size (and attached behaviors) of the hypermasculine/gay body as a source of power (as an agreed protocol in given circumstances), has a somewhat mutable existence within a range of (irreducible) spaces. Within this limited discussion of spaces and powers, we find a dominant theme bleeding across and through varying sets of relations: male homosexuality is being played out through a powerful yet powerless numbers game, and the odds are seemingly (or rather only *appear* to be) in favor of those who "possess" or copy excessively masculine traits.

THE MACHINE DRONES ON

The materiality of language is also expressed in the "stats please" numbers game, which belies its inescapable associations with hypermasculinity in a much broader context. It is tied to a range of language-based metaphors, which construct the male body *and* male desire in highly reductionist and negatively gendered ways. The idea of man in numerical terms again reinforces the man-as-machine trope. As Peter Murphy (2001) points out, the construction of maleness in terms of a machine is limiting and affects not only the way men are thought about but they way they think about themselves. This use of language can then be taken into discussions of "stereotypical" masculinity and negative male "pattern" behavior. Such metaphors, as the title of Murphy's book suggests, are often the metaphors men *live* by. "Cock," "prick," "hard-on," "pecker," and "tool" all contribute to the man/machine construction in language. Murphy (2001:17) writes:

> The most powerful cultural metaphor for masculinity is the machine, a cold, disembodied efficacious piece of equipment . . . True masculinity as a finely tuned, well-oiled, unemotional, hard and cost-effective apparatus deeply informs the way we conceive of manhood, a manhood that, according to Elizabeth Badinter, the French feminist, "is not bestowed from the outset; it must be constructed, or let us say 'manufactured.' A man is therefore a sort of artefact, as such he always runs the risk of being found defective. There may be a defect in the manufacture, a breakdown in the machinery or virility, in short, a failed man."

Murphy (p. 20) traces the origins of the word *cock* within this frame from its use to describe "a spout or tap" that "allows for the flow of wine or cider out of a wooden keg." A cock is also connected to the rooster as a symbol of stridence (resembling a chicken's neck), but in the Caribbean and Southern America cock refers to female genitals, as in "cockles." This demonstrates not only the ambiguity of the term but also the context-specific nature of language as it constructs both gender and sexuality. As a mechanical apparatus that is turned on and off to pour liquids, the word *cock* then renders the penis an "unconscious machine," a "screwing mechanism," or an "insentient tool," and the male body as "engineered to perform a particular task" (p. 21). Murphy argues the male heterosexual (but I would add, quite deliberately, "homosexual") experience is reduced to ejaculation and located "in a dispassionate occurrence of which he is the recipient" (p. 22).

This means the whole notion of the penis as a gay/straight power symbol, not to mention a bulging free pass into sex clubs, is fraught with contradiction and linguistic complexity. Consequently, the penis as a "hard-on" is somewhat ironic, for, as Murphy states, "hard does not describe accurately the quality of the penis even when it is erect" (p. 22). But to think of the penis as other than hard is to admit to fragility, vulnerability, fleshiness, and humanity—so language keeps the artifice of certain ideas about masculinity in place, ideas easily and explicitly reproduced (or parodically copied) within homosexual public/private contexts. And so it is with the often-derogatory usage of words such as *prick* or *tool*. Murphy (2001:33) tells us:

> The male body as a machine with the penis as a tool robs a man of the wonder he can experience when his body becomes a polymorphous organism with a variety of erogenous zones and areas of sexual experience. The machine drones on, in contrast to the body, which sings harmoniously.

The "stats please" command/greeting can thus be understood as the failure of language to adequately facilitate and articulate an experience of the gay male body, which is especially obvious in discursive constructions of male sexuality and sexual performance.

In analyses of pornography, for instance, the somewhat anxious, parodic nature of the "gay masculine" (and the body as machine) remains conspicuously absent. Generally such anxiety is thrown into theoretical relief by a blinding celebratory rhetoric of the queer and the perverse (as in McKee's, 1999, "Suck on that mate"). With respect to porn "made by gay men for gay men," Brian McNair (1996: 103) comments that "in so far as it celebrates and articulates 'deviance,' subverts and challenges still dominant homophobic culture," gay porn becomes "a political text." Similarly, Merck (1993:217) finds that

> gay pornography, like any other forms of representation, includes work distinguished by misogyny, racism and homophobia, as well as invitations to non-macho identifications, satire of heterosexuality and safe-sex information.

However, the political and social importance of gay porn, although possibly demonstrative of the "productive" nature of homophobic power, as Foucault might say, still exists in tension with the fairly obvious exclusory and imitative practices from which the "stats please" greeting/command is drawn. And though invitations to the nonmacho may exist, in titles such as *Gang of 13, A Night with Strangers,* and *Guys Who Suck Big Cocks,* it is certainly difficult to find them. In fact, the one thing equally as valuable in a hypermasculine sense is not just having a humongous penis (attached to a hard, muscular, machine-like body), but being able to take it "like a man." The men doing the giving and the taking in these films are the "stats please" ideal personified, objectified, and ephemerally satisfied.

We return again then to an anxious, if not desperate, "parody of the *idea* of the natural and the original" (Butler, 1990:31), anchored as it is in the limitations of the physical, the essentialist, and the constructivist. The only aspect identifiably "queer" from a political perspective is the male-to-male sex. Conversely, as a set of acts, this queerness is paradoxically conditional; the "gay" sex is something the bodies of "blokes" or "boys" usually perform as part of the buddy/gang function. As Sedgwick (1990:264) has argued, the threat posed by certain acts being attached to identity "can only be exacerbated by the insistence of gay theory that the discourse of acts can represent nothing but an anachronistic vestige." The "str8acting" framing of the gay male body as a robotic sexual machine lessens the possibility that it will it "sing harmoniously" and remain hard at the same time; the stats simultaneously favor a "masculine" body/character and devalue the "alternative, experimental possibilities" of a "politics of difference" (Grosz, 1994:31-32) for gay men.

QUEER AS WHO?

The real problem perhaps in this particular sense is how the "queer" might be reconciled with idealized modes of masculinity, which are in essence exclusive. In such contexts the application of queerness in itself becomes problematic. Like the "stats please" protocol, with its suggestion of male "gayness" as something that can be (or should be) located, measured, or declared, certain brands of queerness when mobilized thus are working within rather than against the "gay/masculine" numbers game which demands some form of definition and value in relation to both mythological and lived practices of masculine extremes.

Recent media representations of gay men witness the relocating (or reclaiming?) of the term "queer" in the face of its theoretical/philosophical usage promoting inclusiveness and the "taking on of the transgressive" (Case, 1991:2). Both the British (1998-2000) and American versions of *Queer As Folk* conflate "queer" solely with "gay" (generally men, with a couple of women thrown into the mix), and this textually and spatially located version of homosexuality is not necessarily seen as incompatible with its epistemologically liberating potentialities. Gauntlett (2002:87) sees the series as the antithesis of the Tom Hanks film *Philadelphia* as "gay men are actually allowed to be seen as interesting and funny and different—and not having to imitate middle-class, middle-aged heterosexuality in order to be accepted." Charges that representations of gay men in the series are unrealistic or "not normal enough" are dismissed as implying "the three (very different) central characters in the drama should be compelled to represent an average, blanded-out spirit of uncontroversial gayness" (p. 150). Compared with the American sitcom *Will & Grace* (1998–), *Queer As Folk* (and the U.S. series in particular) has an explicitly transgressive approach to identity and sexuality. In *Will & Grace* the "outrageous queen," Jack, begs Will to put the "sex" back into "homosexual," which of course he can never do in prime-time, mainstream TV space, but which the boys (and women) from *Queer*

As Folk do every week and then some in their late-night, limited-release programming slots.

The narrative of *Queer As Folk* adds some interesting elements to an understanding of the mimicry and spatial identities inherent in the "stats please" mind-set. The series starts with the story of a teenager (Nathan/Justin) who is literally seeking out a gay space in the throbbing gay districts of Manchester/Pittsburgh, respectively. He is picked up by the Stuart (UK)/Brian (US) character (an attractive, successful, sexually predatory advertising executive) and his initiation into the gay "scene" begins. Like everyone else, the teenager becomes obsessed with the elusive "A-gay." He learns sets of protocols from him which he quickly puts to use—such as the emotionally distancing line to ward off morning-after emotional advances from one-night stands: "I've already *had* you. . . ." He eventually begins a "proper" relationship with him, based on a series of rules regulating the conditions of their promiscuity. As the *Queer As Folk* characters move from the gym to the backroom, the bedroom to boardroom to schoolroom to showroom to the nightclub and the diner, their friendships withstand numerous trials, but a sense of emptiness prevails—gay men's relationships generally don't last, and when they do it is because no one says what they really want from them. In the U.S. series, the younger Justin is visibly shattered when the emotionally unattainable Brian gives him his birthday present—a picture "perfect" male prostitute lying on a bed with a bright ribbon tied around him—a reminder of the sexualized macho ideal which unites them and others under this version of "queer"; their relationship is a joint subscription to the numerically declared and to the unspoken. Speech, or articulation of thought, is where the real problems begin. The other central character of the U.S. version, Michael, has fast and furious sex with a physically "perfect" man he has met on the Internet moments after his relationship with a chiropractor has fallen apart. Michael repeatedly tells the man he is perfect. At the end of the session the man tells Michael that he too could become perfect (the perfect "gay masculine") if he would have some work done, just like he did—pectoral implants, cheek implants, dental work, and, of course, a penis extension. Michael later says the guy spoiled the encounter by opening his mouth. The personification of the stats (as numbers, not words) sustains the (preferable) possibility of pleasure through silence. Framed in space by the bed, the television screen, and the computer monitor the numbers add up—they are easily reproduced—but lose any signs of the messiness inherent in sex acts, identification, and communication.

Though it may seem that these slick and showy accounts of "same-sex" activity symbolize an attempted essentialist trapping of queerness, such examples again tell of the mimic and of male gayness as a form of self-modification, renovation, and maintenance. The dual functions of endorsing and undermining gay "masculine" idealization coexist. This in itself could be interpreted as a critique of gay/queer culture to some extent. However, through the clothes, the clubs, the music, the bodies, and the "style" attached to gayness, this recent version of the TV queer can also be seen to encourage the commodification of qualities that can be disinvested from their association with gay male sex. American production house Bravo TV's recent successful reality program *Queer Eye for the Straight Guy* places gay male queerness precisely in the context of a commercially attainable set of traits. A group of gay men work on different aspects of a straight man to make him over through their "queer" eyes:

> They are the Fab 5: an elite team of gay men who have dedicated their lives to extolling the simple virtues of style, taste and class. Each week their mission is to transform a style-deficient and culture-deprived straight man from drab to fab in each of their respective categories: fashion, food and wine, interior design, grooming and culture. It's a full lifestyle make-over—a *make better* show where straight guys turn in their pleats for flat fronts, learn about wines that don't come in a jug and come to understand why hand soap is not a good shampoo (and vice versa). When the journey is done, a freshly scrubbed, newly enlightened, ultra hip man emerges. (*Queer Eye,* 2003)

Queer Eye for the Straight Guy places male homosexuality squarely on the side of the hip, the camp, and the beautiful, just as unproblematically as *In and Out* (1995) attached it to excessive hygiene and an obsession with Barbra Streisand. So the stats come out to play—gay men with style-perfect bodies and hair, and the smoothest dance moves, tidy up and "enlighten" their less fortunate heterosexual counterparts. In one scenario, through expert tutelage, the target "straight guy" has lost 100 pounds and is ready to learn how to shake his thing on the dance floor. The trajectory generally works to see the rough edges removed, as the statistical perfection of the body is eventually affirmed by its attachment to (or assimilation to) social spaces and practices.

Interestingly here, a particularly class-oriented version of male homosexuality becomes the copy to be copied. So is this a revolutionary win for the side of queer, or a heterosexist commercial exploitation of a "less-than-masculine," pan-homosexual subjectivity? Michael Idato (2003) writes in *The Sydney Morning Herald:*

> When the series launched in the US, some in the gay community were uncomfortable with its overt stereotyping, despite the exposure it gave to gay men. There are parallels with the way America's black community has struggled to get more black faces on TV while avoiding such stereotypical roles as hookers, pimps and drug dealers . . . Doesn't it represent an acceptance of homosexuality in mainstream American society? Certainly there are some in the US media who believe the show has broken the taboo on homosexuality in American broadcasting culture, but that claim is probably premature. In fact, *Queer Eye* is far more camp than it is gay, much like *Will & Grace*, the fairly anodyne sitcom about a single gay man and his female best friend. When shows like these are hailed as groundbreaking you have to wonder just what Americans think groundbreaking actually means.

If *Queer Eye* reflects the acceptance of gay men within the mainstream, someone will need to explain this to the family of Matthew Shepard, or here in Australia, to the men and women fighting for the acknowledgment of their relationships, access to superannuation, and parental rights in the face of political and religious conservatism. What is acceptable in the public "eye" is the value of this economically "feminized" queerness to an all-encompassing heteronormative discourse of idealism. *Queer Eye,* like Australian reality TV shows such as *Changing Rooms* and *Room for Improvement* (which both use flamboyant gay men as interior designers and decorators) defines the functions, talents, and character traits of gay men within their capacity to entertain a mainstream audience and their roles as "assistants" to heterosexual narratives of advancement. While *The Amazing Race* is testament to the idea that only certain types of (idealized masculine) gay men can "win," the ultimately sexless figures of *Queer Eye* can be relieved of the need to perform hypermasculinity by similarly reinforcing its idealization and its attachments to social structures that ultimately exclude them. As Butler (1990:31) says, gay is to straight as "copy is to copy," but make no mistake as to which copy is more important, which copy is subordinated to the other, and which copy is deemed more "natural."

The common ground shared by gay and straight is not found to be the rigid cultural constructions of masculinity, which have kept them apart for so long, but the act of consumption itself. As each product and label is placed strategically throughout the homes of their "victims," so too is the name of each brand vigorously repeated and reinforced (in one episode, fashion guru Carson works with the "straight guy" to ensure he can finally pronounce Ralph Lauren correctly). As with the "degaying" (and depoliticizing) of the 1980s American gay publication *Details,* the dequeering in *Queer Eye* can be framed in the following way:

> ... certain style conscious corporations and their allied ad agencies soon realized that such a sensibility, stripped of its political content, could be a Trojan horse. From its belly might come the images that would turn a nation of young men into colonies of slavish male shoppers. (Faludi, 1999:516)

Where the politicized queer subverts boundaries and norms, this commercial one sells an equally parodic image of the straight guy back to himself. In both statistical and economic terms, the value of homosexual mimicry and redefinition in space (and its own appreciation of the masculine ideal) are granted a currency here, though they are hardly "queer" in the sense of "the open mesh of possibilities" which work outside of "monolithic signification" (Sedgwick, 1993: 18).

The net result of these representational processes is that one must now dig even deeper, and quarry selectively, to find the theoretical possibilities within such constructions. This "reality" quite consciously serves to reinforce the idea of performance, which underscores the relationship between the phrase "stats please" and the gay male body in physical and virtual spaces. In the first episode of *Queer As Folk* the Brian/Stuart character is marvelled at by his male friends. They watch him effortlessly identify then procure the most attractive gay men in any given situation. He dances around them, brings them closer, then leans in and whispers something those watching him can never quite make out. "If only we knew what he says," one of them sighs. "Those magic words," another adds. Maybe there are no words, just numbers—stats if you like (such as those that measure the penis or the chest, or those that measure "queer" in terms of commercial success). This might be what makes him so enticing yet so repelling, so knowable yet unknowable, so obvious, yet undefinable and elusive. As Foucault (2000:140) said, "we must think that what exists is far from filling all possible spaces. To make a truly unavoidable challenge of the question: What can be played?" The spatial power of the "stats please" protocol could actually be in what it hides rather than what it declares. The seeking out of a measured, imagined masculinity might well be undone by the very imperfection of the copy, the inexplicable lure of those unimaginable differences of the gendered outcast, which the numbers can never fully conceal. Watch this space.

REFERENCES

Barker, C. (2000). *Cultural studies: Theory and practice.* London: Sage Publications.

Block, The (2003). "Official Website," available at http://www.ninemisn.com.au/theblock.

Butler, J. (1990). *Gender trouble: Feminism and the subversion of identity.* London: Routledge.

Caillois, R. (1984). Mimicry and legendary psychasthenia, J. Shepley (trans.). *October,* 34:17-32.

Case, S. (1991). Tracking the vampire. *Differences: A Journal of Feminist Cultural Studies,* 3(2):1-20.

Casey, M. (2003). A taste for Jamie. NEWS.com.au, August 28, available at http://entertainment.news.com.au/common/story_page/.

Faludi, S. (1999). *Stiffed: The betrayal of modern man.* London: Vintage.

Foucault, M. (1980). *Power/knowledge: Selected interviews and other writings 1972-1977.* New York: Pantheon.

Foucault, M. (1986). Of other spaces. *Diacritics,* 16:22-27.

Foucault, M. (1993). Space, power and knowledge. In S. During (Ed.), *The cultural studies reader* (pp. 161-169). London and New York: Routledge,

Foucault, M. (2000). *Essential works of Foucault 1954-1984: Ethics,* P. Rabinow (Ed.). London: Penguin.

Gauntlett, D. (2002). *Media, gender and identity: An introduction.* London: Routledge.

Grosz, E. (1994). Identity and difference: A response. In P. James (Ed.), *Critical politics: From the personal to the global* (pp. 29-33). Melbourne: Arena Publications.

Grosz, E. (1995). *Space, time and perversion: Essays on the politics of bodies.* New York: Routledge.

Idato, M. (2003). Pride or prejudice? *The Sydney Morning Herald,* September 29, available at http://www.smh.com.au/articles/2003/09/28/1064687667152.html.

McKee, A. (1997). Fairy tales: How we stopped being lesbian and gay and became queer. *Social Semiotics,* 7(1):21-36.

McKee, A. (1999). Suck on that mate. In D. Verhoeven (Ed.), *Twin peeks: Australian and New Zealand feature films* (pp. 119-126). St. Kilda: Damned Publishing.

McNair, B. (1996). *Mediated sex: Pornography and postmodern culture.* London: Arnold Ltd.

Merck, M. (1993). *Perversions: Deviant readings.* London: Virago.

Mirzoeff, N. (1999). *An introduction to visual culture.* London: Routledge.

Murphy, P. (2001). *Studs, tools and the family jewels: Metaphors men live by.* Madison: University of Wisconsin Press.

Queer Eye for the Straight Guy (2003). "Official Website," available at http://www.bravotv.com/Queer_Eye_for_the_Straight_Guy/About.shtml.

Sedgwick, E.K. (1990). Axiomatic. In S. During (Ed.) *The Cultural Studies Reader* (pp. 243-268). London: Routledge.

Sedgwick, E.K. (1993). *Tendencies.* Durham, NC: Duke University Press.

Chapter 7

Narcissism, the Adonis Complex, and the Pursuit of the Ideal

Daryl Higgins

> I got no emotions for anybody else
> You better understand I'm in love with my self
>
> > "No Feelings"—Sex Pistols

> Narcissus is a symbolization of the existential unfulfillment with respect to the longing for contact and union. Narcissus is unable to unite with the other, with himself, or with anyone else, and this human condition creates his existential suffering. (Hermans & van Gilst, 1991:437)

In this chapter, I will use the Greek myths of Narcissus and Adonis as tropes—or metaphors—to help understand the vagaries of self-concept and interpersonal attraction in gay men. I want to ask some provocative questions (drawing on the perspectives of critical psychology, social constructionism, and discourse theory), such as whether narcissism is our punishment for failing to return the affection of our brothers, and whether pursuit of an ideal leads ultimately to disenchantment and disappointment. I will also explore whether the lack of legal and sociocultural practices to support same-sex partnerships and the perceived short-term nature of many relationships can result in—or be the result of—body obsession and self-absorption. Rejection of others because of narcissistic self-absorption or idealizing and

---

*I am grateful to the editors, Wayne Martino and Christopher Kendall, and to Alan Wilson for their invaluable feedback and constructive critque on earlier drafts of this chapter.

striving to attain an unrealistic embodiment of masculinity—the Adonis—both lead to an unhealthy focus on the body. In this chapter, I will explore how both of these complexes (represented by Narcissus and Adonis) create the body as a site for affirming our masculinity and trying to attain the unattainable. I will explore the notion of how masculinity (or masculinities) is constructed, as well as the impact this has on the embodiment of masculinity in gay men's lives. Finally, I want to explore the relationship between masculine representations, body absorption, and the notion of community. Does sex—and our sexuality—isolate us, or does it lead us into community?

At a wedding reception I attended recently, someone tried to explain the relationship between two men who were neighbors of the mother of the bride.

> "They're friends," she said.
> "Friends of whom?" I asked.
> "Of themselves."

I presumed she was using "friends of themselves" as a euphemism for the men being gay/lovers/partners—a love whose name she dared not utter. However, the words she chose to use are noteworthy: she said "friends of *themselves*," rather than "friends of *each other*." Was this an innocent malaprop, or a signifier of a deeper suspicion that attraction of a man to another man is a subterfuge for his inherent narcissism? Is this what we are condemned to be: friends of ourselves, rather than of each other? Are same-sex-attracted men to be seen as those who have rejected the affections of women and now are stuck with being "friends of themselves"? This social praxis is an example of how sexuality is constructed as a consequence of the binary of the heterosexual/homosexual matrix (Angelides, 1995).

To understand how same-sex-attracted men can be seen as self-absorbed, attempting to find a mirror of themselves, it is necessary to consider how "the homosexual" is constructed as the Other. Within the binary logic of a heterosexual/homosexual matrix, identification can be achieved only by excluding the Other. The Other gets constructed within heteronormative frames of reference. Gay men must be distinguished from straight men, and men who choose not to be in a relationship with a woman must be attempting to relate to themselves (see Fuss, 1991). In contrast to the man/woman coupling epitomized by the bridal couple whose relationship we were celebrating, the man/man coupling could not be named; yet it served to stabilize and reify the essentialist, primordial expression of heterosexuality: "Homosexuality is produced inside the dominant discourse of sexual difference as its necessary outside . . ." (Fuss, 1991:5).

Examination of the psychoanalytic understandings of narcissism is useful if we see it as a means of theorizing how social processes, such as the socialization into gender and sexual orientation categories "interpenetrate the workings of the psyche" (Henriques, Hollway, Urwin, Venn, & Walkerdine, 1984:208). Henriques et al. (1984) argue that:

> because of the particular ways in which psychoanalysis links sexuality with the unconscious, it is directly implicated in any attempt to understand the forms and possibilities of change in personal life. (p. 207)

We see how regulatory practices and discursive frameworks constrain identity, and define the parameters and content of desire, and its expression. Foucault (1990/1976) noted that homosexuality became a "species."

> Homosexuality appeared as one of the forms of sexuality when it was transposed from the practice of sodomy onto a kind of interior androgyny, a hermaphrodism of the soul. The sodomite had been a temporary aberration; the homosexual was now a species. (Foucault, 1990/1976:43)

It was no longer just a description of behavior, but a way of defining individuals; not just an act, but a personage:

> There is no question that the appearance in nineteenth-century psychiatry, jurisprudence, and literature of a whole series of discourses on the species and subspecies of homosexuality, inversion, pederasty, and "psychic hermaphrodism" made possible a strong advance of social controls into this area of "perversity"; but it also made possible the formation of a "reverse" discourse: homosexuality began to speak in its own behalf, to demand that its legitimacy or "naturality" be acknowledged, often in the same vocabulary, using the same categories by which it was medically disqualified. (Foucault, 1990/1976:101)

Rather than rely on essentialist notions of identity, Henriques et al. (1984) set forward a nondualistic approach to subjectivity that accounts for the production of social differences. They argue that cultural practices "are not simply overlaid upon a pre-existent desire but actually help to produce the fixing and channelling of desires by virtue of their production of power-knowledge relations" (p. 203).

Hollway (1984b) pointed out the potentially contradictory nature of discourses that are available for subjects to take up, and the need to question "how it is that people take up positions in one discourse rather than another" (p. 237). She also demonstrates how responses to simple things such as test items on a personality inventory are dependent on circumstances and contextual factors, highlighting the "contradictory constructions of subjectivities" (Hollway, 1984a:46). The development of the identity (or "species") of the homosexual/ gay man, and its positioning within the binary framework of heterosexual/homosexual, highlights the crucial difference around which the identity label is centered: the love of the "opposite" sex (borrowing from the gender binaric), which is seen as normative, versus the love of one's own gender, which is seen as deviant, signaling the gay man as the Other. Gay men are constructed as the Other through their supposed rejection of the necessary complementarity of essentialist notions of gender (see Angelides, 1995). This also presupposes that all men "naturally" are attracted to women, and that an innate biologic imperative is consciously being rejected!

THE MYTHS OF NARCISSUS AND ADONIS

Are gay men by definition narcissistic, because they take themselves—their own gender—as a sexual love object? Many people misunderstand the myth of Narcissus,[1] thinking that its purpose is to show that when we become obsessed with the self, particularly physical attractiveness (often in a highly gender-stereotypic sense), we fail to see and reach out to others. However, an alternate reading could demonstrate the reverse sequence of causality. Narcissus's self-obsession—gazing at his own reflection in the pool—was his punishment for rejecting Echo and the other nymphs, allowing him to feel what it was like to love and meet no return of affection: to fall in love with the self. It is not that self-obsession leads to isolation, but rather that the punishment for rejecting others is self-obsession.

Psychoanalysts have found the myth of Narcissus to be fertile material for explaining the primal autoerotic drive observed in humans. Freud used it to develop his (rather negative) theory of the development of homosexuality. According to Freud, homosexuality results from a boy's "failure to abandon sufficiently quickly his own body, especially his genitals, as a libindinal object. Later in life, his choice was therefore of a person with genitals similar to his own" (Macmillan, 1997:358).

Freud theorized that narcissism (and its outworking—autoeroticism) is a primal phase from which all individuals need to progress. However, when fixated in this normal developmental stage, social instincts become sexualized, leading to a homosexual object choice. Narcissistic adult-love relations are the feminine form of love, as it relies on the aim of being loved: being the object (or the phallus) of desire. Drawing on the work of French psychoanalyst Jacques Lacan, recent psychoanalytic feminists also understand narcissism in terms of the ego taking itself as its own libinial object (e.g., see Grosz, 1990; Henriques et al., 1984). Homosexuals (or "inverts," as Freud terms us) "proceed from a narcissistic basis, and look for a young man who resembles themselves and whom *they* may love as their mother loved them" (Freud, 1905b:144, n. 1, cited in Macmillan, 1997:338). This does not necessarily rely on oedipal longings, but in fact is deeper: the preoedipal, infantile narcissism is transferred onto the other (the mother) in order to love himself (Grosz, 1990).

Another manifestation of self-obsession and striving to reach perfection can also be understood by what is known as the "Adonis complex": the fixation that some men have with the idealized body. Adonis was a particularly beautiful youth whose beauty captivated even the gods. As the epitome of masculinity/male perfection, he easily captures our attention, and we, too, want to become like him. But it is not so easy for everyone to live up to what can be an unrealized ideal: the toned, muscular, athletic body. Forrest (1994) highlighted that

> the emergence of the male body as a "desired" and "objectified" commodity [seems] to have produced a certain recentring of the masculine arena. We may be witnessing the proliferation of certain identities based on sexual practices, fashion, life-styles or certain fetishes, but these revolve around the *athletic male body*. (p. 104)

How are images of the masculine ideal created and promulgated? The role of media in creating—and reflecting back to society—an image of the male to which we can aspire needs to be considered. The relationship between the media and male subject as consumer is complex in the representation of the idealized male form. The ritualized body becomes the inscription for one's social location and position. According to Grosz (1995), the body is inscribed by "cultural object-signs." For example, Forrest (1994) wrote about the London gay scene and the bodily representations of gay men:

> Gay men, it now seems, are going to the city's gyms in droves. In virtually all gay erotica and in the advertisements for gay chat-lines, escorts, and bars and clubs, macho posturing, bulging biceps, sculpted pectorals and lashing of torn denim, black leather and sports gear appear to be the norm rather than the exception. (p. 97)

The media do not simply impose such body norms and ideals. In a sense, gay men actively deploy such technologies to fashion particular embodied masculinities. As Forrest (1994) noted, such representations of gay men are not as straightforward as they appear: "Gay men still behave in 'unmanly ways'" (p. 97). Despite the apparent alignment with archetypal modes of masculinity, he suggests two behaviors signify a paradoxical departure: the love of drag and the desire to be fucked.

> Whatever its contradictions or changing characteristics, "male masculinity" is tied to a masculine body. This body is hard, muscular and athletic; a symbol (if not a guarantee) of power within a hierarchically gendered society. (pp. 104-105)

Consumers are incited to appropriate Adonis masculinities because of the promise of having their masculinity assured in a society that relies on the binaries of male/female, feminine/masculine to regulate social behavior and sexual desire. Personal desires are not constructed outside of such social forces. The politics of gender and the politics of sexual orientation are interlinked. Both categories are not fixed, immutable categories, but are socially constructed (Rahman & Jackson, 1997). Adoption of an identity category "male" and/or "gay" involves the individual in an interaction with socially prescribed and reified signifiers of those identities. A complex interaction exists of developing and reinforcing bodily texts and the performatives of maleness and gayness. The Adonis image is one such demarcation, one which has currency in defending against the equation of homosexuality and femininity. If male equals power within patriarchal societies, and the quintessential signifier of male is an idealized version of the hard, athletic, muscular physique, a gay man's assertion of his masculinity through the sculpting of his body is a means by which to eradicate all vestiges of the feminine:

> Gay men may be attracted to different degrees of masculine expression, of which the body is just a part. But by enhancing our physical "manliness" we have done much to dilute the myth of our "womanly" and inferior nature. Yet through our "masculinization" are we not also reinforcing the very gender categories which are frequently the source of that oppression? (Forrest, 1994:105)

ATTACHMENT AND MASCULINITY

From a Freudian or Lacanian perspective, narcissism is seen as an immature sense of self, which results from not receiving adequate "mirroring" (or affirmation) from the main caregiver in infancy (see Grosz, 1990). If we did not develop a sufficiently secure attachment to our caregivers in infancy because we experienced rejection or felt only intermittently valued (i.e., they were insensitive or unresponsive), we are likely to develop an insecure attachment style characterized by avoidance or ambivalence (see Bowlby, 1969; Carver, 1997). Although attachment styles have their origin in infancy, they are believed to continue into adulthood, influencing adult relationship styles (Alexander, Feeney, Noller, & Hohaus, 1998). Romantic partners operate as attachment figures for each other. If a body feels shamed while growing up and rejected by a potential attachment figure, he may seek out a relationship or encounter to relive this drama and complete his "unfinished business." Often this experience of rejection and poor attachment occurs with fathers—many of whom do not know how to relate to a son who may not conform to gender stereotypes of masculinity (including heterosexuality). Early experiences of being shamed for engaging in nonconforming gender behavior (e.g., playing with dolls, dressing up in women's clothes, preferring quiet activities to sport or aggressive games) can leave a gay son without appropriate affirmation.

What options does such a son have? To reject the father or idealize the missing attachment figure and what he symbolizes: masculinity. The psychoanalytic concept of "attachment" explains the relationship between loss and narcissism. Kohut (1991), a neo-Freudian psychoanalyst, outlined his notion of the *selfobject:* it refers to the infant-caregiver bond, but also to objects experienced as part of one's self. Kohut described immature narcissism as the individual longing for connection with an idealized parent. This can continue into adulthood, when a partner (who may be substituting for a parent in providing a nurturing bond) fails to affirm the narcissistic self's exhibitionistic demands, resulting in shame. Kohut's view was that:

> narcissistic vulnerability may occur, frequently resulting in grandiosity expressed as unrealistic expectations of self. Clients show this through self-criticism or condemnation for not achieving unrealistic goals. Thus, there is a constant overwhelming sense of guilt and shame at this failure to achieve and a longing for connection with an idealized parent. (Brown, 2004:44)

Kohut argued that "the grandiose self that does not receive mirroring or affirmation from the main caregiver, does not achieve a mature sense of self" (Brown, 2004:44). Narcissism represents the failure to meet some ideal or failure to fully connect with another (Brown, 2004).

SHAME, MASCULINITY, AND VIOLENCE

Given the link between masculinity and sense of self in males, shame experienced by gay men is likely to be experienced in relation to our gendered selves: the inability to live up to heteronormative ideals of the masculine. Failure to live up to this ideal (and the reminder of this through homophobic practices and polemics) engenders shame. Brown (2004) elucidated the link between attachment, shame, and violence. The experience of poor attachment—or, in Kohut's terms, and inadequate selfobject—leads to feelings of shame. Shame is not a pleasant emotion, one that males in particular are socialized to avoid.

Brown claimed that some men use anger to minimize the experience of shame. Shame is an immobilizing and passive emotion. It strikes at the core of masculinity. Shame is associated with effeminacy. A common way by which men try to avoid shame—and the resulting emasculation—is through the assertion of power and exhibitionism. One arena in which this is played out is the physical body: an over-idealization of the body as the site of power. The obsessive desire for muscles and a hypermasculine appearance provides an insulating shield against the shame of appearing nonmasculine (i.e., nonheterosexual) in our heteronormative world.

Gay men are often targeted with the label "effeminate" because of our lack of conformity to stereotyped gender roles and heteronormative models of masculinity. However, this is because the dominant heteronormative culture facilitates the social construction of gender as binary opposites. Given the integral relationship between gender and sexuality, such a gender binary is then superimposed on the hetero–homo divide (Rahman & Jackson, 1997). Any transgression of gender norms established within heteronormative culture immediately results in an inscription of a deviant sexuality. As Fuss (1991) noted:

> Homosexuality, read as a transgression against heterosexuality, succeeds not in undermining the authoritative position of heterosexuality so much as reconfirming heterosexuality's centrality precisely as that which must be resisted. (p. 6)

Shame is associated with effeminacy. In order to avoid shame, "effeminate" men—not all of whom are gay—may try to avoid the shame through power and exhibitionism. Overidealizing the masculine, an embodied hypermasculinity is seen as the ultimate goal: the Adonis complex. The heteronormative culture that produces such regimes of embodied masculinity means that identity categories themselves tend to become instruments of regulatory regimes (Butler, 1991). Shame is produced as a result of certain normalizing practices that get legitimated in the dominant culture: bifurcation of gender performativity regulates the behavior, and shame is a mechanism of social control to support the hierarchical distinction. The obsessive desire for more muscles and hypermasculine appearance is to wear an insulating shield against the shame of being nonmasculine/nonheterosexual (it is the same, isn't it?).

Although the body is a principal site for reifying masculinity, there is a range of subtle manifestations of the Adonis complex/body obsession. Power and status are sought for—and symbolized—through the right label, or the right look in cars, clothes, and other commodities. Having the right haircut and waxing the right parts of your body show that you cut it. Masculine power is expressed through money as well as muscles.

Feelings of inadequacy about our masculinity lead to shame and/or fear of being perceived as effeminate. The heteronormative environment, in which most of us grew up, makes living with such feelings of shame intolerable. And so we do something about it. Often we reassert masculinity through violence. Heterosexual males often engage in violence against women in order to overcome feelings of shame (Brown, 2004). Domestic violence is also an issue in gay relationships, where masculinity and power can still be asserted through violence (Island & Letellier, 1991). Gay men sometimes turn the violence on themselves, punishing their bodies to conform to an ideal, engaging in drug taking, gruelling partying, excessive dieting, and internalizing homophobic attitudes—letting seeds of self-deprecation grow. But it is not just the way we punish ourselves; it is also the expectations we have for others.

Does a gay man need a classically beautiful (i.e., a godlike Adonis) partner in order to feel acceptable to himself? A beautiful partner "mirrors" to the individual his ideal of masculine beauty, whether or not he lives up to his own internalized standard of perfection. Narcissism is quite different from self-love. Health promotion experts, psychologists, and self-development experts encourage people to "look after themselves," to develop a positive self-image, and to have a healthy self-esteem. The emergence of *metrosexuals*—heterosexual males who, like the stereotype of gay men, look after their appearance and are not afraid of face creams and exfoliating body scrubs—emphasize the importance of self-care for men. But attached to this is the risk of idealizing a certain look that for many is unattainable: wanting to be the beautiful youth Adonis.

The problem is not just for those with an Adonis complex, trying to attain an impossible ideal of masculine beauty, but also for those who seemingly are the ideal: the narcissists. But even for Narcissus, his perfect beauty did not save him. Narcissism includes the elements of suffering and punishment. Narcissus initially perceived the image in the pool as being that of another person. He was drawn into continual suffering by being unable to drag himself away from the image in the pool, despite now knowing that it was his reflection. Narcissus rejected the affirmations of Echo and her fellow nymphs; however, it was from his own reflection in the water that he experienced rejection. It was the answered prayer of the rejected maiden, who had prayed that Narcissus might one day feel what it was to love but not receive any affection in return. Although mesmerized by his own image, Narcissus's experience is analogous to rejection or self-hate: he was rejecting himself. It is from his own image that affection is not returned. This was his punishment for rejecting others.

The lack of affection from parents and our peers while growing up—a lack of affirmation for who we were as young gay adolescents—may be the force that drives us to the waters of the clear fountain and to become fixated with the image we see reflected. Narcissism is an "unfulfilled desire for unity with one's self and with the other" and "a longing for contact and union with somebody or something else . . . that is not fulfilled" (Hermans & van Gilst, 1991:423, 435). The key component is lack of fulfillment. We need to consider how the hegemonic representations of gender and sexuality combine to create a narcissistic obsession with self-image as a mechanism for social inclusion, a means of obtaining affirmation and acceptance from the cultural group of gay communities.

BODY IMAGE

The focus on the body and the desire to conform to an ideal type can be pathologized as a neurotic regression: an infantile reaction formation against the way we fear we are (i.e., inadequate). However, it could also be seen as a cause for celebrating the freedom for men to be attracted to what turns them on. For some, this is plucked, preened, hard-bodied men. For others, it is something closer to the reality of twenty-first century urban life: men no longer spend all day physically running around trying to capture food or defend their physical territory. We do these things on a psychological level—yet we want the physical body that would suggest we physically live our lives this way (or even if we cannot manage it for ourselves, we are turned on by men who achieve this ideal). To compensate, we need to push boundaries at the gym and fight battles with ourselves at the dinner table or the snack bar.

The Adonis complex and obsession with body image means that men are now muscling in on what was seen as the almost exclusive domain of women: body image disturbances and eating disorders (e.g., anorexia and bulimia). And we go to great lengths to do it, including obsessive gym use and abuse of steroids. The goal is to remove all unsightly hairs and all visible body fat, chisel our physiques, and cover it in a glossy, golden, all-over tan. Does a hard body provide the promise (or the hope) of a hard cock? Steroid abuse and the subsequent atrophy of genitals and gonads give the lie to this.

The result is sham masculinity, a facade. It is a representation of masculinity that takes considerable effort to create, and left unattended, would falter. It involves drugs (steroids), indoor activities (weight and circuit training), shaving, waxing, clipping, and tanning. All fragments of natural manhood (such as facial and other bodily hair) are removed in order to fully expose the facade that surrounds the frightened body: afraid of being seen as "girlie," which is the ultimate insult.

But it's not just gay men; in the straight world too, men are obsessed with their bodies and the things they need to do to keep in shape: "Where once men got a sense of self-worth and esteem through the workplace, now they're working out in gyms and guzzling down steroids in hot and dangerous pursuit of the perfect body" (Landeman, 2000:15). The rising interest in fashion, grooming, and the use of cosmetics by men—homosexual or "metrosexual"—can be seen as evidence of the importance of the body to men. However, it can also be seen as the site for contestation, the boundary between gay and straight. Again, with heterosexuality as the norm, and culturally defined modes of expressing masculinity, straight-acting masculinities are often eroticized, even within gay circles (Forrest, 1994). The athletic male body is the center of many identities. Forrest asks "*why* such 'masculine' characteristics (however ambiguous and contradictory) have been desired, adopted and consciously reinforced by gay men" (p. 103). He sees the answer tied up in hostility toward the feminine. In highly gendered societies, he argues, it is not surprising that "gay men wish to be seen as 'real men'" (p. 103).

> Women's associated gender characteristics—such as gestures, concerns, dress, mannerisms, language and the like—are seen as inferior ways of behaving, regardless of whether they are taken on by a man or a woman. (Forrest, 1994:103)

However, the pursuit of an ideal "masculine" body type can be dangerous. The stereotyped image of the buffed, bronzed, and pumped man with a square jaw and piercing blue eyes is attainable only for a few. Extreme diet and exercise can be damaging to men's health. And the pursuit of this unrealistic and somewhat artificial ideal can isolate gay men from others around them. The body becomes the site for competition, and for the losers in the race the object of shame and self-loathing. Instead of reaching out and connecting—spiritually, mentally, emotionally, and physically—with fellow gay brothers, ritualized activities (dieting, exercising, tanning, waxing) can be a distraction from the primal need for connection and intimacy with others.

As gay men obsess about hardening their bodies, do they fail to see their common humanity with other gay men, who may not be afraid of expressing their femininity? They also run the risk of hardening their hearts to their own need for community and communion.

Is narcissism a self-produced condemnation—and a way of enforcing a constricted and constrictive mode of being gay on the individual himself—and on others? Despite its facile superficiality, many still love the buffed and preened look (or at least you'd think so, if you look at any gay magazine or the podium dancers at a gay club). But not all do. Gay communities encompass a variety of idealized forms, not all of which valorize muscular, toned young men. But within various subcultures such as the Bears, the feminized Other gets inscribed and denigrated. Intrahierarchical relations get played out on all levels with straight-acting masculinities getting legitimated and eroticized as the norm. Communities have grown up around alternate modes of dress and being, including leather, facial and/or body hair, and the larger body size ("Bears") and their admirers ("cubs"). However, some of these alternate communities involve elements of body worship (piercings, tattoos, fetishized clothing or accessories) that still focus the attention on an embodied masculine ideal. For many, it is an external image that is never complete or perfect, and therefore never ultimately satisfying.

Are we products of commercial media interests? The men's fashion industry (targeted to a considerable extent at gay men) creates images of the hyperbeautiful and the fetishized body: airbrushed and digitally enhanced. (Although a recent advertisement perhaps signals a reversal: the latest advertisement for Yves Saint Laurent's fragrance "M7" features a full-frontal nude male covered in body hair—an unusual sexualizing of the natural-looking male body, and for some, I suspect, a breath of fresh air and a reprieve from the self-imposed (yet media-fueled) demand for the smooth, sculptured look. However this presents yet another ideal to which we can aspire (and fail) to live up to. These images are part of a complex interplay of the channeling and regulation of desire, and its mobilization through media and cyber technologies.

Forrest (1994) concluded his discussion of the changing nature of gay male identities in the United Kingdom by looking at the notion of gay community and its nexus with the commercial:

> For most gay men a sense of community has always been centred on a commercial scene—pubs, clubs, bookstores, porn movies and so on . . . Our sense of a gay community is increasingly determined by commercial interests. (p. 108)

Drawing on the work of Altman, he argued that such commercialization of community and the reinvention of the gay identity as a consumer facilitate the integration of gays into mainstream society. Similarly, I would argue that notions of community in which inclusion is based on representations of gay men as "hypermasculine" (in order to shore up their identities as "male") has a double edge: it may serve to bolster the inclusion of gay men in the gendered hierarchy of "male," but at the expense of those who fail/choose not to live up to such an ideal/oppressive image.

What happens at the level of community is likely to be a reflection of what happens on the individual, intrapersonal level. I want to turn to an examination of the preferences gay men express in terms of their own partnerships. Maybe the gay man's desire for a particular image is just about what turns him on. Why do different traits turn us on? Is it just a random thing, or can we discern a pattern in the attractions of gay men? How do the hegemonic heteronormative representations of masculinity relate to attraction and desire, and the types of partnerships that gay men form?

WHAT DO GAY MEN PREFER IN A PARTNER?

A number of factors can affect a gay man's object choice (the type of man to whom he is attracted). I believe one factor is how same-sex-attracted men come to understand themselves as particular kinds of gendered beings or "subjects." When gay men lack a clear sense of their own masculinity and feel inadequate, they are likely to internalize society's negative attitudes, and seek to make up for the perceived lack. Homophobia represents an attack on the feminine in all men, but particularly gay men (see Forrest, 1994).

Psychological theories of interpersonal attraction have been developed in the context of nonsexual friendships between males and females. Can they be applied to understanding the nature of gay attraction and whether they seek similarity or complementarity in their relationships? Are gay men attracted to "like" or "opposites"? Do we want someone who shares similar characteristics? Or are we looking for someone who has complementary traits, attitudes, or physical attributes that make up for our self-perceived inadequacies? Psychologists have typically explained interpersonal attraction in terms of similarity: people are attracted to others who are similar to themselves, in terms of shared attitudes, values, life experiences, demographic history, et cetera. But is this what gay men look for? Are we—like heterosexuals and like Narcissus—content (or condemned?) to gaze on someone just like ourselves? However, not all of us are as happy with our appearance and ourselves as was (we assume) Narcissus. What if we feel inadequate in our sense of masculinity—or our degree of muscularity (one of the defining features of masculinity)? Do we subscribe to the Adonis masculinity in attempting to fashion ourselves in the very image of the male that we ourselves find attractive? The pathogenic effects of internalized homophobia can interrupt the process of healthy identity formation. If a gay man assesses himself as being masculine but introjects the social stigma toward gay men—particularly "feminine" gay men—he may consider only "masculine" men to be attractive. Alternatively, if he has come to accept his identity and disregards the hegemonic guidelines of "heterosexual masculinity," then he may feel comfortable in preferring a male partner who has "feminine" qualities.

In heterosexuals, interpersonal attraction has been explained in terms of similarity—however, this usually is measured in terms of

similarity of attitudes and life experiences, in the context of friend-
ship, rather than romantic/erotic attraction. Research on gay men's
preferences for "masculine" appearance or "psychological" masculinity in partners has focused on ideal partners. Bailey, Kim, Hills, &
Linsemeir (1997) found that a small subgroup of "femmes" (effeminate gay men) were just as likely to prefer "butch" (masculine) men
as to prefer femme men. Boyden, Carroll, & Maier (1992) found that
gay men rated their ideal partner as being logical, expressive, and of
similar age and masculinity–femininity to themselves. We extended
this by conducting a study looking not only at *ideal* but *actual* partners, and the similarity between these and the respondents' perceptions of themselves: both how they currently see themselves *(actual
self),* and how they would like to see themselves *(ideal self).*[2] Overall,
I found support for a "similarity" hypothesis with regard to the ideal
partner. Their ideal partner was similar to how they saw themselves
(actual self). However, for the subgroup of respondents with an actual
partner, a different picture emerged. Actual partners were *not* rated as
similar to either their ideal self or their actual self. So, although a gay
man's ideal partner may be similar to how he sees himself, those with
partners suggest that actual partners do not necessarily reflect this
ideal (Higgins, 2004). Although gay men may be seen—like Narcissus—to be gazing after someone who reflects their own ideal self-
image, the men they end up connecting with in relationships may not
necessarily be the same as how they themselves, or how they would
ideally like to be.

Many gay men report that their *ideal* partner is similar to how they
would *ideally* like to be themselves and—to a lesser extent—how
they *actually* see themselves now. It seems that we search for ourselves in a partner (our *ideal* partner) but may fail to find this (our *actual* partner may not match our ideal). Does this explain—at least in
part—the reported short-term nature of many gay relationships? Our
attempts at seeking perfection in our partners can blind us to a potential partner's good qualities. Do we, like Narcissus, reject others?
Maybe the punishment for seeking the ideal man—the perfect coupling—is our isolation from real men around us and the risk that we
become self-absorbed. Searching for Mr. Right may dull our hearing
to the point where we ignore the faint echo of our brothers' pleas for
connection. Is narcissism and its consequences our punishment for
failing to return the affection of others?

LESSONS FROM THE STORIES
OF NARCISSUS AND ADONIS

Whether we reject others through our self-absorption (narcissism) or whether we long to become an idealized version of masculinity (the Adonis complex), the end result is the same. The body becomes fetishized: the site for affirming our masculinity, or trying to attain the unattainable, the site of longing and self-punishment. What is the alternative? Maybe it is about reframing our capacity for self-reflection in a positive way. Homosexual desire and gay love do not have to be defined by self-absorption. In fact, I would argue, love is how it is overcome. Narcissism and the Adonis complex have in common a difficulty in connecting with others in a real way. We become obsessed with ourselves, or with others (trying to be someone that we are not) instead of realistically trying to develop human connection and relationships.

Quality relationships with others require moving beyond looking skin deep when we look at the embodied gay man. I believe the lack of accepted rituals within the gay community for promoting and supporting partnerships contributes to body obsession and self-absorption. Too often we see sex as an achievement (an opportunity for exploitation), rather than an act of communion. Choosing to have a sexual encounter with someone physically arousing (or who will fill your need for someone to find you arousing) may be a fun experience; however, it may not be the best way to find a long-term partner. Such partnerships require connection at a level other than just the physical—and may require modifying or letting go of unrealistic or unhelpful ideals for ourselves and others. Many different ways of developing real community and connection between people exist, and gay men are at a point in history where different modes of being and connecting with one another are opening up.

The lack of legal supports and sociocultural practices and rituals for gay partnerships can also contribute to a focus on sex and the body. The life-giving power of a relationship based on compatibility of personality and the capacity to feed the soul of the other becomes secondary. Civil registration of partnerships, social/religious celebrations, legal access to partners' superannuation, and other symbols of equality with heterosexual couplings may assist gay men in moving away from identity politics based on a discourse of difference (from the other: the heterosexual) to an assumed equality of all relationships, regardless of gender/sexual orientation. In the meantime, sex and the personal embodiment of sexuality can become for some a compensation for the cultural limitations on gay partnerships. Angelides (1995) expressed his concern with identity politics, pointing out how it relies on binary oppositions in order to mobilize action; yet this of itself shores up the boundaries between the discourses it should contest: it leads to a "reinscription of the essentialised identities contained within its borders" (p. 37) by relying on the "artifice of binary difference" (p. 38).

Ideals are not bad per se. However, it depends on what is being idealized. Ideals based on an "illusory binary difference" mean that "identification is achieved only through the exclusion of the Other" (Angelides, 1995:28). Ideals that are available to most heterosexuals—legal marriage, biological children, extended family support—are not always available to gay people. I argue that we should find our own positive ideals: ones that are not limited to the body and that move us closer toward our brothers. And sex can be an important part of that communion with the Other. Sex can move us beyond our isolation: the narcissistic self-absorption or frenetic attempts to match an external ideal—the Adonis. Our ideal should not become disconnected from the physical—disembodied—but recognize that love and connection are more important than physicality alone.

For those of us who are physically aroused by members of the same sex, the perceived societal proscription against expressing love and desire for another male makes autoeroticism and narcissism an easier option than risking harassment and prejudice by seeking what we want in a homophobic culture and being who we are. Many gay men "do not know how to love either themselves or each other, for it is difficult not to demean or exploit others in turn when one is oneself irrationally despised by society at large" (Frontain, 2002). The purpose of sexuality is to connect human beings. As one commentator reflected in his critique of Terrence McNally's controversial play *Corpus Christi,* sex should be about communion, not exploitation: it is "a redemptive sharing of one's body with those whom one loves" (Frontain, 2002:235). The purpose of sexuality is to connect human beings.

NOTES

1. Narcissus—the son of a god—was a beautiful youth. Many young men and women found him attractive, but he turned them away. A nymph called Echo wanted to tell Narcissus that she loved him but could not, as she could only repeat what was said to her. One day Narcissus became separated from his companions while walking in the woods. He called out, "Is anyone here?" Echo replied, "Here, here." Echo ran forward, ready to put her arms about his neck. "Hands off!" exclaimed Narcissus. "I would rather die than you should have me." She retreated to a cave, and there is nothing left of her but her voice, ready to reply to anyone who calls her. An avenging goddess heard and granted the prayer of the rejected maiden, who wanted Narcissus to feel what it was to love and meet no affection in return. As he stooped to drink from a clear fountain, he saw his image and fell in love. He could not tear himself from his image and eventually pined away. From where his body lay, a flower grew which bears his name. He lost his humanity but retained his self-love and his beauty. See Thomas Bulfinch, *Mythology: The Age of Chivalry* and *Mythology: The Age of Fable* (in Martin, 1991) and D. A. Leeming (1990), *The world of mythology*.

2. The aim of this study was to investigate how theories of interpersonal attraction developed in relation to heterosexuals would explain whether gay men would prefer partners with gender traits (masculinity, femininity, and attitudes toward muscularity) that are similar to their own. A sample of gay men in Australia ($n = 90$) completed a self-report survey. The results demonstrated a significant positive correlation between the characteristics of an *ideal* partner and the characteristics of both the *ideal* self and *actual* self. No significant relationship was found between the *ideal* or *actual* self and *actual* partner. The similarity of traits was associated with attraction to an *ideal* partner but not to an *actual* partner.

REFERENCES

Alexander, R., Feeney, J., Noller, P., & Hohaus, L. (1998). Attachment style and coping resources as predictors of coping strategies in the transition to parenthood. Paper presented at the Australian Institute of Family Studies, Melbourne, November 25-27.

Angelides, S. (1995). Rethinking the political: Poststructuralism and the economy of (hetero)sexuality. *Critical inQueeries, 1*(1):27-46.

Bailey, J. M., Kim, P. Y., Hills, A., & Linsemeier, J. A. W. (1997). Butch, femme, or straight acting? Partner preferences of gay men and lesbians. *Journal of Personality and Social Psychology, 73:*960-973.

Bowlby, J. (1969). *Attachment and loss,* Volume 1: *Attachment.* New York: Basic Books.

Boyden, T., Carroll, J. S., & Maier, R. A. (1992). Similarity and attraction in homosexual males: The effects of age and masculinity-femininity. In W. R. Dynes & S. Donaldson (Eds.), *Homosexuality and psychology, psychiatry, and counselling* (pp. 13-22). New York: Garland Publishing.

Brown, J. (2004). Shame and domestic violence: Treatment perspectives for perpetrators from self-psychology and affect theory. *Sexual & Relationship Therapy,* *19:*39-56.

Butler, J. (1991). Imitation and gender insubordination. In D. Fuss (Ed.), *Inside/out: Lesbian theories, gay theories* (pp. 13-31). New York: Routledge.

Carver, C. S. (1997). Adult attachment and personality: Converging evidence and a new measure. *Personality and Social Psychology Bulletin, 23:*865-883.

Forrest, D. (1994). "We're here, we're queer, and we're not going shopping": Changing gay male identities in contemporary Britain. In A. Cornwall & N. Lindisfarne (Eds.), *Dislocating masculinity: Comparative ethnographies* (pp. 97-110). London: Routledge.

Foucault, M. (1990/1976). *The history of sexuality,* Volume 1: *An introduction* (trans. R. Hurley). London: Penguin.

Frontain, R. (2002). All men are divine: Religious mystery and homosexual identity in Terrence McNally's *Corpus Christi.* In R. Frontain (Ed.), *Reclaiming the Sacred: The Bible in gay and lesbian literature* (pp. 231-257). Binghamton, NY: Harrington Park Press.

Fuss, D. (1991). Inside/out. In D. Fuss (Ed.), *Inside/out: Lesbian theories, gay theories* (pp. 1-10). New York: Routledge.

Grosz, E. (1990). *Jacques Lacan: A feminist introduction.* Sydney: Allen & Unwin.

Grosz, E. (1995). *Space, time and perversion: The politics of bodies.* St. Leonards, Australia: Allen & Unwin.

Henriques, J., Hollway, W., Urwin, C., Venn, C., & Walkerdine, V. (Eds.) (1984). *Changing the subject: Psychology, social regulation and subjectivity.* London: Methuen.

Hermans, H. J. M., & van Gilst, W. (1991). Self-narrative and collective myth: An analysis of the Narcissus story. *Canadian Journal of Behavioural Science, 23:*423-440.

Higgins, D. J. (2004). Partner characteristics and preferences in gay men: The role of self-perceptions. *In preparation.*

Hollway, W. (1984a). Fitting work: Psychological assessment in organisations. In J. Henriques, W. Hollway, C. Urwin, C. Venn, & V. Walkerdine (Eds.), *Changing the subject: Psychology, social regulation and subjectivity* (pp. 26-59). London: Methuen.

Hollway, W. (1984b). Gender difference and the production of subjectivity. In J. Henriques, W. Hollway, C. Urwin, C. Venn, & V. Walkerdine (Eds.), *Changing the subject: Psychology, social regulation and subjectivity* (pp. 227-263). London: Methuen.

Island, D., & Letellier, P. (1991). *Men who beat the men who love them: Battered gay men and domestic violence.* Binghamton, NY: Harrington Park Press.

Kohut, H. (1991). *The Search for the Self,* P. Ornstein (Ed.), New York: International Universities Press.

Landeman, C. (2000, May 15). Adonis complex: The new obsession. *The Age,* p. 15.

Leeming, D. A. (1990). *The world of mythology.* New York: Oxford University Press.

Macmillan, M. (1997). *Freud evaluated: The completed arc.* Cambridge, MA: The MIT Press.

Martin, R. P. (1991). *Bulfinch's mythology: Introduction, notes and bibliography.* New York: HarperCollins.

Rahman, M., & Jackson, S. (1997). Liberty, equality and sexuality: Essentialism and the discourse of rights. *Journal of Gender Studies, 6:*117-129.

Part II:
When Gender Harms
and Oppression Becomes the Norm

In this part of the book, four gay men discuss, with courage and without holding back, what hierarchies *do* and what can happen to those of us who either take the sexual role models we are offered seriously or dare to reject them. Analyzing the effects of pornography, domestic violence, and male rape, these men bring to light the reality of gender oppression and speak as the outcasts they have needed to become to survive. What they search for in these writings is an opportunity to challenge the oppression caused by inequality and sexualized gender hierarchies. The model presently on offer does little more than sexualize a role-play that often rejects compassion, affection, and equality between gay men and that instead promotes, through sex, homophobia and sexism, self-hate, hate for others, and harm to others.

In Chapter 8, Christopher Kendall looks at the links between gay male pornography, male rape, and domestic violence. Kendall argues that the effects of gay male pornography are no less damaging than the effects of heterosexual pornography. On the contrary, gay male pornography encourages male dominance. Because it glorifies the masculine and denigrates the feminine, gay male pornography reinforces the male/female social dichotomy and hierarchy. Within this context, Kendall argues that gay male pornography strengthens those stereotypes that allow society to view certain behavior as feminine, and hence inferior. In this sense, it can be read as reaffirming that it is "unnatural" to engage in a sexual dynamic not premised on male/female polarity. It is argued that it can often result in legitimating those actions and practices which make homophobia and sexism a threat to physical safety and social equality.

In Chapter 9, Rus Ervin Funk asks what being raped says about being a man, and then proceeds to expose the world in which that question is answered. By offering the voices of those who have been traumatized through sexual assault, Funk explicitly reveals queer men's relationship with masculinity and the harms that result when this relationship is not questioned or rethought. Discussing the extent to which gay men who are raped as part of gay bashing, Funk then highlights the silence surrounding the issue of date rape for queer men. He argues that queer men who are raped by a date or spouse often not only do not receive support from within the community, but often are explicitly told to not talk about the incident. The queer male community seems not only extremely reticent to discuss the issues, but also unwilling to offer support to gay and bi men who are sexually assaulted.

In Chapter 10, Peter Shuttlewood brings to light the trauma of gay male domestic violence. Allowing us to view firsthand the experiences of those who have been victimized by those who profess to care for them, he addresses the questions asked but rarely answered: why it happens, why victims stay, what masculinity tells us about the role of those who abuse and those who are abused, and why silencing is the norm in a community that denies the reality of harm and intra-community ignorance about violence and the sexualization of abuse that is so clearly gendered. By denying the experiences of those who are fortunate enough to escape and tell their story, the gay community creates the role of "outcast" and strives for conformity in which hypermasculinity is the norm. Sadly, the effect of enforced masculinity is not questioned, leaving some alienated and without a community.

Finally, in Chapter 11, Simon Obendorf examines the sexual objectification of Asian men in gay male pornography. Exposing the fusion of race and gender and the codification of racially based sexual desire, Obendorf analyzes those pornographic materials in which Asian men are sexualized, primarily for the benefit of non-Asian men. In this context, feminization is central to the presentation of gay Asian men, such that it combines with race to support the entrenched marginalization of nonwhite men through a process of sexual disempowerment. This is best evidenced in magazines such as *Oriental Guys*, often defended by pro-pornography advocates as "liberation" or "central to gay male equality." Obendorf highlights how the effects of these materials on gay men's perceptions of themselves and other men should not be underestimated. The cover of magazines such as *OG* promise the reader "positive images of Asian men." As Obendorf explains, the contents speak otherwise, making inequality the norm.

Chapter 8

Pornography, Hypermasculinity, and Gay Male Identity: Implications for Male Rape and Gay Male Domestic Violence

Christopher Kendall

INTRODUCTION: ARGUING FOR AND WINNING "THE RIGHT TO PRIVACY"

On June 26, 2003, in the case of *Lawrence v. Texas,* the United States Supreme Court overruled a Texas sodomy law on the basis that gays are entitled to respect in their private lives. Following a long line of privacy cases going as far back the 1973 abortion decision in *Roe v. Wade,* the Court held that, with respect to laws that outlawed gay male sexual relations, "the state cannot demean their existence or control their destiny by making their private sexual conduct a crime" (Greenhouse, 2003). And so, at least in the United States, gays and lesbians continue to celebrate their newfound freedom—the freedom to be "left alone" in the privacy of their homes.

In this chapter I ask the question: What exactly are we celebrating? Although I for one recognize that my partner and I should be allowed to engage in consensual sexual activity without worrying about the police knocking down our door and throwing us in prison, to limit the privacy analysis argued in court by gay rights advocates to this kind of state-based harassment is quite simply naive. More important, it risks ignoring the very real harms caused to real people in the private sphere. In other words, what one does in private still needs to be subjected to some form of scrutiny and critical practice that is committed to interrogating harmful behavior.

To make my point, I intend in this chapter to discuss privacy within the context of gay male rape and gay male domestic violence—two issues that too many of us have chosen to ignore but which are central to any "celebration" of the right to do what one wants in the privacy of one's own bedroom. I will do so within the context of gay male pornography—an issue that cannot be separated from any privacy analysis and one which, like privacy, seems to be taking up a lot of time on the part of gay male litigants and academics keen to defend it in court as something all gay men should be able to use as they see fit. This is an argument that I will reject as a clear violation of the sex equality interests we *should* be fighting for—instead of shortsighted legal battles that aim to convince the courts that we can do whatever we want in private.

My overall argument will be that gay male pornography promotes violence and aggressive, nonegalitarian behavior. Its message, what it promotes, is hypermasculinity found at the expense of some else's liberty and self-worth. Merit is found in degradation, and rewards are attached to one's ability to use or be used. Equality, if present at all, is found only in reciprocal abuse. And the extent that the "right to privacy" is used to justify the "private" will, for many of us, *not* be a safe space. Until we recognize this and refocus our litigation and personal struggles toward a more equality-based model of liberation, serious issues of inequality and harm will remain intact—with liberation and social progress simply cast aside.

THE PRIVATE SPHERE: THE PROBLEM WITH BEING "LEFT ALONE"

Gay Male Rape

In his brilliant analysis of gay male rape, Michael Scarce (1997) argues that gay men are more likely to be raped than straight men, and gay men are more at risk of being battered by their same-sex partners than their heterosexual counterparts. Scarce notes that in a 1989 study by psychologist Caroline Waterman at the University of Albany, 12 percent of 34 men in gay relationships "reported being victims of forced sex by their current or most recent partner" (Waterman and Dawson, 1989:118). Similarly, in another study researchers found that gay college students reported significantly higher lifetime prevalence of sexual victimization than did heterosexual men participating in the same study (Duncan, 1990). Finally, in a study of 930 gay men living in England and Wales, 27.6 percent reported they had been sexually assaulted at some point in their lives (Hickson, 1994:281). Studies elsewhere support these conclusions (Calderwood, 1987; Mezey, 1992; Goyer and Eddelman, 1984).

Domestic Assault

Of America's 9.5 million adult gay men, 350,000 to 650,000 are victims of gay male domestic violence in the United States each year. That makes gay male domestic violence the third largest health problem facing gay men in the United States today (Island and Letellier, 1991:1). We can no longer ignore it. Applying these statistics, only substance abuse and AIDS adversely affect more gay men.

The Privacy Factor

So what, you are thinking, does all of this have to do with privacy? Well, a lot actually, much of which cannot be discussed in this chapter. What can be discussed, however, is pornography—pornography as a privacy right, pornography as a central cause of both gay male rape and domestic violence. It is a link conveniently swept aside in *Lawrence v. Texas* (2003), but one which needs to be addressed before any more bottles of champagne are opened.

YOUR "PRIVACY"/OUR HISTORY— WHATEVER HAPPENED TO SEX EQUALITY?

As a Canadian, I am always a bit wary of telling Americans they have screwed up. But, well, sometimes the truth needs to be aired. Gays now have privacy in the United States. In Canada, we have this other concept called sex equality. Big difference. Especially when it comes to pornography and what it says about rape and sexual violence.

As Stoltenberg notes, "the privacy principle really blazed into the libertarian limelight with with *Stanley v. Georgia* in 1969, in which the US Supreme Court ruled that *a man* may legally possess obscenity in his home" (Stoltenberg, 1990:121), resulting in the catch phrase "a man's home is his castle." Note the emphasis on "man." I'll come back to that in a minute.

In Canada, pornographers tried a similar argument in 1992, in the case of *R v. Butler*. Fortunately, rejecting the privacy argument, the Canadian Supreme Court chose instead to recognize pornography for what it is: a violation of every Canadian's constitutional right to sex equality. The Court held that

> [t]he effect of [pornographic] material is to reinforce male-female stereotypes to the detriment of both sexes. It attempts to make degradation, humiliation, victimization, and violence in human relationships appear normal and acceptable. A society which holds that egalitarianism and non-violence are basic to any human interaction is clearly justified in controlling any medium which violates these principles. (*R v. Butler,* 1992:493)

Although not explicitly stated by the Court, this definition of pornographic harm closely resembles an earlier definition of pornography first articulated by American feminists Catharine MacKinnon and Andrea Dworkin. In 1983, long before the Supreme Court of Canada was asked to tackle the constitutional validity of Canada's laws, Dworkin and MacKinnon drafted a civil rights ordinance for the City of Minneapolis aimed at addressing the real, specific acts directly caused by the production and distribution of pornography (Dworkin and MacKinnon, 1988:21). The ordinance was designed to stop those materials that injure the public welfare by violating and discriminating against women and gay men. Their goal was to eliminate pornography as a systematic practice of exploitation and subordination that is central in creating and maintaining sexual inequality. Under the ordinance, which was not ultimately passed in the United States except for Indianapolis, Indiana, due to the U.S. Constitution's obsession for free speech protections—something Canadian courts have rejected as secondary to equality interests—pornography was defined as follows:

> *Pornography* shall mean the graphic sexually explicit subordination of women, whether in pictures or in words, that also includes one or more of the following:

1. Women are presented as sexual objects who enjoy pain or humiliation; or
2. Women are presented as sexual objects who experience sexual pleasure in being raped; or
3. Women are presented as sexual objects tied up or cut up or mutilated or bruised or physically hurt, or as dismembered or truncated or fragmented or severed into body parts; or
4. Women are presented being penetrated by objects or animals; or
5. Women are presented in scenarios of degradation, injury, abasement, torture, shown as filthy or inferior, bleeding, bruised, or hurt in a context that makes these conditions sexual; [or]
6. Women are presented as sexual objects for domination, conquest, violation, exploitation, possession, or use, or through postures or positions of servility or submission or display.

The use of men, children, or transsexuals in the place of women . . . shall also constitute pornography. (MacKinnon, 2001: 1517)

Materials that fit this definition were not banned by the ordinance but were made civilly actionable as sex discrimination when the acts of coercing a person into performing for pornography, forcing pornography on a person, assaulting a person due to specific pornography, and trafficking in pornography were engaged in.

Redefining pornography as a sexually discriminatory act, rather than a point of view, mere text, or simple idea likely to cause offense, this radical redefinition sought for the first time to allow those harmed by pornography's inequality and sexual exploitation to prove their injuries and, in so doing, take action to stop those responsible from continuing to hurt them and others. It is this definition of pornography to which I refer when I use the term *pornography* throughout this chapter. It encompasses all materials that at their core sexualize inequality through gender hierarchy.

Now what, you are all thinking, does all of this have to do with *Lawrence v. Texas?* Well, as I see it, *Lawrence* leaves the claim wide open to gay men to now argue that they, like straight men, have the right to produce, distribute, access, and use pornography in their home—that castle now guaranteed for all American men. Well . . . all except perhaps those of us who have been subjected to sexual or physical or psychological violence of the sort produced in a society in which male supremacy is the norm and in which inequality is sexualized by those most keen to enshrine privacy as a constitutional right.

And don't assume it won't happen. Again, the Canadian context serves as a valuable source for learning about what can happen when gay men see and then defend pornography as a right, a source of liberation, a source of pride, something central to the formation of a positive gay male identity.

On December 20, 2000, the Supreme Court of Canada ruled in the case of *Little Sisters Book and Art Emporium,* a case concerning the right of Canada Customs to detain lesbian and gay male pornography, that lesbian and gay male pornography violates the sex equality test for pornographic harm first set down by the Court in its 1992 decision in *R v. Butler.*

In the *Little Sisters* case, Little Sisters Bookstore, and many of the Interveners that supported it, rejected the claim that same-sex pornography could result in the types of harms that result from the distribution of heterosexual pornography. The Court disagreed, finding that gay male pornography, like heterosexual pornography, results in the types of physical and social harms that make racism, homophobia, male supremacy, and misogyny normal and a violation of the right to equality that all citizens have the right to enjoy.

The remainder of this chapter examines the claims made in *Little Sisters* that gay male pornography is "different" from heterosexual pornography, that it is harm-free and a right worth fighting for. I do so within the context of gay male rape and gay male domestic violence—issues that have received little analysis by gay male writers, either before or after the *Little Sisters* case. I do so because I am convinced that before long similar claims will be made in the United States and elsewhere—on the basis of this new right to privacy. I want to argue that, to the extent that this *is* the case, we should all be worried, particularly if you care about those in our community silenced by sexual violence—violence done in private, often because of the pornography that many gay advocates, lawyers and academics will end up defending, intentionally or unintentionally, as a privacy right (read now, thanks to *Lawrence:* a gay male right).

Let's return to *Little Sisters.* The central argument used in that case by gay rights advocates was best summarized by the Appellant, Little Sisters Book and Art Emporium, who wrote:

There is solid academic criticism of the equation of homosexual pornography with mainstream heterosexual pornography. Erotica produced for a homosexual audience does not and cannot cause the kind of anti-social behavior generally or through stereotyping and objectification of women and children that Parliament apprehended might be caused in heterosexual obscenity. While heterosexual obscenity is often misogynist, that cannot be said of homosexual pornography. (Little Sisters Factum, 1999, paras. 48 and 63)

Similarly, EGALE Canada, who intervened on behalf of Little Sisters, argued that

sexually explicit lesbian, gay and bisexual materials challenge the dominant cultural discourse. They resist the enforced invisibility of our marginalized communities and thereby reassure us that we are not alone in the world, despite the apparent hegemony of heterosexuality. They reduce our sense of isolation. They provide affirmation and validation of our sexual identities by normalizing and celebrating homo- and bi-sexual practices, which mainstream culture either ignores or condemns. In short, they help us feel good about ourselves in an otherwise hostile society. (Factum EGALE, 2000:7)

Feel good about ourselves? Really? Unlike most of the groups who defended *Little Sisters,* I actually took the time to look at these "sources of liberation" defended so forcefully as lifesaving, empowering, and inclusive. Let me try to summarize them. Most of what follows were the actual court exhibits defended at the trial. Because the materials in question had been deemed illegal in Canada, the summaries that follow were read and dictated by me into a tape recorder over a two-day period in a locked room in the British Columbia Court of Appeal, Civil Exhibits Division, Vancouver, in October 1999. I was not allowed to photocopy any exhibits because they had been deemed illegal, and they are now inaccessible because of the Supreme Court's ruling. Any errors in dictation and transcribing are entirely my own.

If the materials defended in *Little Sisters* indicate the gay identity defended by pro-pornography and pro-gay advocates, as they say they do, what has the Supreme Court of Canada just been told about homosexual identities? In answering this question, it is worth noting the quotations below, found in an article in *Little Sisters* Exhibit 198 before the Supreme Court, *Advocate Men* (1989). Like many of the materials defended in *Little Sisters* they remind the reader that to be "male" is to be empowered, but that to be male requires conformity to a clearly defined gender norm—a gender role according to which some are entitled to sexually abuse and control, while others, because they are descriptively less "male," are socially less relevant, less equal, and not entitled to the respect, compassion, and human dignity that only true equality can provide. This particular story, titled "The Plan," describes a young man in drag (a transvestite). It details how he is sexually used by an older man (who is not a transvestite). The story draws a clear distinction between who is and is not the "man" in the sexual relationship and outlines what it takes to fit either the masculine or feminine role. In one quote, the nontranssexual says to the transsexual male:

> What you want is me putting you on your knees. You want me stuffing money down your bra and fucking your face until cum runs down your chin while you are creaming your panties. You want fancy motel rooms and big double beds and my meat rammed up your ass. You want drive in movies with petting and kissing and my dick in your mouth. You want to be a lady and a tramp right?

At one stage, the younger man is forced to have sex in public. When he explains that he is worried about what people might see and say, the older man says, "Fuck em. You're my cunt. Not theirs."

As in a great deal of written or pictorial gay male pornographic presentations, what one gets from the previous scenario is a "source of affirmation" in which the physically more powerful, ostensibly straight male is glorified. The linking of manliness with heterosexuality and overt masculinity is a common theme throughout many of these materials, with masculinity often gained at the expense of a woman or ostensibly gay male's safety and self-worth. The misogynistic overtones in these materials are clear.

The same edition of *Advocate Men*—a magazine modeled along the lines of *Playboy* and *Penthouse* magazines—features men who are youthful, muscular, or well toned and includes a number of photo spreads of the type of men often used in these magazines. The article that accompanies one of these collections of photographs reads:

The first thing people notice about Glen Fargus, apart from his stern masculinity and animal sexuality is those muscles of his. It is easy to resent him when he remarks that he has never lifted weights but all is forgiven when Glen gives the reason for his physique. "I like to fuck a lot," he says. He is described as working as a foreman and although this requires a lot of heavy lifting, this is nothing compared to "the work I put into pumping some young stud's butt." . . . "Sometimes my muscles get me in trouble. Some guys say I'm too rough during sex. I get into it and all the other guys end up all bruised. Like they say, no pain no gain." (*Little Sisters* Trial Exhibit 198, 1989:66)

An article in the same magazine, "Perfect Husband," tells the story of a young gay man's attraction to another (married—read "non-gay") man who is described as "so hetero it's unbelievable." Jack (the married, heterosexual man) is described in terms that make it clear that he is a "real" man in this relationship. We are told, for example, that he cannot cook because that is his wife's duty and forte. The story describes Jack having anal sex with his young gay male companion. The gay man is described performing oral sex on his straight friend, with Jack saying to this man, "You were right . . . Men are better at it than women and a mouth has no sex. You know I don't feel any guilt at all. It's great" (*Little Sisters* Trial Exhibit 198, 1989:26).

Similar themes to that in "Perfect Husband" are emphasized in the next story in the same magazine. Titled "Night Watchman," this story describes a gay man who has a number of sexual experiences with married men. One quotation from that article describes one non-gay male encouraging another non-gay male to rape a gay man. It reads:

Now, fuck that hard ass man he told me yanking my cock hard and placing it against his hole. Shove that big cock up there until he screams. Fuck him man, you know how bad he wants it. Just do it until he screams and you load him full of cream. (*Little Sisters* Trial Exhibit 198, 1989:39)

The article continues:

"The man's got a tight, tight pussy man," Phil told me. He wrenched his hand free and slapped Saul in the back. "Lean over

> and show this man your pussy ass." (*Little Sisters* Trial Exhibit 198, 1989:40)

Frequently, sexual subordination is enforced through extreme forms of torture and violence, with masculinity again epitomized and celebrated in men who ridicule and emasculate others in the name of sexual pleasure. Those who are emasculated in these materials are often specifically described as gay males, while those who abuse them and who are iconized as sexual role models are described as straight, read "real," men.

What these examples provide is a sexualized identity politic that relies on the inequality found between those with power and those without it; between those who are dominant and those who are submissive; between those who are top and those who are bottom; between straight men and gay men; between men and women. From these and other materials, we are told to glorify masculinity and men who meet a hypermasculine, muscular ideal. The result is such that men who are more feminine are degraded as "queer" and "faggots" and are subjected to degrading and dehumanizing epithets usually used against women, such as "bitch," "cunt," and "whore." These men are in turn presented as enjoying this degradation. In sum, they reinforce a system in which, as MacKinnon explains, "a victim, usually female, always feminized" is actualized (1989:141). Insofar as sex equality is concerned, the result is the promotion and maintenance of those gendered power inequalities that reject a nonassimilated gay male sexuality and which ensure that homophobia and sexism remain intact (Pharr, 1988).

Throughout many of these materials rape is normalized. Consent is implied. In the story "Sucks Brother Off Before Wedding" from *Juice: True Homosexual Experiences,* for example, the writer describes being raped by his older brother when he was eight and a half and the joy he experienced at being the source of his brother's anger and sexual violence. Explaining that this formed the basis of his preferred sexual experiences in adulthood, the reader then details another of his sexual encounters as follows:

> Once when I was about 25 I got raped by a powerful young guy that I had taken home to blow. I always say that was the best sex I ever had. Rape at that stage of the game was enjoyable. God he was good. He knew just what to do to a willing asshole that kept

saying no. He took me with force and I fought him right to the bitter end and—thank God—he won out. When he got through with my asshole I knew I had had it. The bastard never came back though. (*Little Sisters* Trial Exhibit 213, 1984)

The identity sold in these materials is one in which violence by one man against another man or men is presented as sexual for the persons involved and for the consumer of these materials. It is a common theme. The magazine *Dungeon Master—The Male S/M Publication,* for example, a magazine that would have been freely imported into Canada if *Little Sisters* had had its way, presents men torturing other men in sexually explicit ways with hot wax, heat and fire, while sexualizing this abuse as sexually arousing for the abusers, the persons injured, and, again, for the consumer. The magazine *Mr. S/M 65* presents photographs of men being defecated on and who derive pleasure from eating and drinking excrement. The film *Headlights and Hard Bodies* includes footage of men sexually using other men who are being pulled by neck chains, hit and whipped while tied to poles, penetrated by large objects, and/or subjected to clamping, biting, and pulling of their nipples and genitals. Men presented as "slaves" are shown in considerable pain but finding sexual enjoyment from the abuse inflicted on them by others. Those released from bondage kiss the man or men who beat them and thank them for putting them in their place with whips and verbal degradation. *Mach* magazine, in turn, glorifies sexually explicit torture in a military setting, while detailing the kidnapping, torture, and sexual mutilation of prisoners of war. In a photograph in the same magazine, two young men are shown confined in a cage. One, face down and bent over, is being slapped by an older man in a Nazi military uniform. Another is chained and hung in stirrups with a hand shoved down his throat.

What one sees in these and other examples of gay male pornography is an almost pervasive glorification of the idealized masculine/male icon. Cops, truckers, cowboys, bikers, and Nazis are eroticized; racial stereotypes are sexualized and perpetuated; muscles, "good looks," and youth are glorified; and ostensibly straight (or at least "straight-acting") men beat, rape, and/or humiliate descriptively (frequently stereotypical) gay men. Sadism, bondage, water sports, fisting, bootlicking, piercing, bestiality, slapping, whipping, incest, branding, burning with cigarettes, torture (of the genitals and nipples, with hot wax, clamps, and the like), child sexual abuse, rape, and prison rape are presented as erotic, stimulating, and pleasurable. In most, if not all, of these materials, it is the white, physically more powerful, more dominant male who is romanticized and afforded role model status. In those scenarios where male sexual partners "take turns" being the "top," the characteristics of dominance and nonmutuality remain central to the sexual act. In those photos where men are alone, positioned, posed, humanity is removed and replaced with an object. As "Men Against Rape and Pornography," a U.S. activist group accurately explain, the man exposed becomes a nonhuman, an object waiting for you to do something to it or wanting to do something to you because he has what it takes to do so (Men Against Rape and Pornography, 1993). The message sent is that some people want and deserve to have sex forced on them. They solicit this and they deserve this. Either way, the result is a sexuality that is hierarchical and rarely compassionate, mutual, or equal. This was the conclusion first offered by LEAF in its submission to the Supreme Court in *R v. Butler* in 1991. Specifically, in summarizing the materials before the Court in that case, the Women's Legal Education and Action Fund (LEAF) argued:

> Some of the subject materials present men engaging in sexual aggression against other men, analogous to the ways women are treated in the materials described above. Men are slapped with belts. A man is anally penetrated with a rifle. Men are presented as being raped. Men's genitals are bound. They are in dog collars and in chains. Men lick other men's anuses and are forced to lick urinals during anal intercourse. Men are presented as gagging on penises down their throats. Men urinate on men and ejaculate into their mouths. Boys are presented with genitals exposed, surrounded by toys. (LEAF, 1991, para. 5)

These materials lead LEAF to conclude that

> Individual men are also harmed by pornography . . . LEAF submits that much of the subject of pornography of men for men, in addition to abusing some men in the ways that it is more common to abuse women through sex, arguably contributes to abuse and homophobia as it normalizes male sexual aggression generally. (LEAF, 1991, para. 48)

An overview of the materials available since *Butler* was first heard reveals that little has changed, other than perhaps LEAF's somewhat disappointing decision to defend the very materials it opposed in *Butler* as sexist, misogynist, and racist.

The materials summarized here, many of which were defended in *Little Sisters* as free of harm and central to gay liberation, provide but a small overview of the content of the types of pornography available to and consumed by gay men. They are, however, indicative of what is used and, if Little Sisters and those who intervened in the case on their behalf had proven successful in their bid to throw out the Supreme Court of Canada's *Butler*-based sex equality analysis of pornographic harm, would now be readily available throughout Canada. These materials and many more.

What these materials typify is the identity that pro-pornography litigants, academics, and activists defend when they seek to strike down anti-pornography legislative regimes on the basis that gay male pornography equals gay male identity. Their effect? What is being advocated in the name of liberation and equality plainly creates, packages, and resells a sexuality that epitomizes inequality: exploitation and degradation of others; assertiveness linked with aggression; strength equated with violence, physical power, and the right to overpower; intimidation, control of others, lack of mutuality, and disrespect; humor found in the sexual debasement of another, and being hurt presented as pleasurable; violating and being violated presented as identity politics; and aggressive, nonconsensual behavior advanced as normal and sexually promoted as liberating. In sum, gay male pornography merges with an identity politics that personifies all that is masculine, hence gender "male," and which rejects all that is nonmasculine, feminized, hence gender "female"—an identity through which, as Andrea Dworkin explains, gay men are not only penetrated like women, but are expected to lust after pain and degradation, much like women are thought to under male dominance (Dworkin, 1974: 89).

BUT IS IT HARMFUL?

The summary of the content of gay male pornography provided in this chapter is indicative of what gay male pornography *is*. Although content and presentation vary in degree and explicitness from one medium to another, what one gets from the previous paragraphs is an overview of what gay male pornography says and does. In arguing as they did before the Supreme Court of Canada that gay male pornography should be exempt from the sex equality standard set by the Court in *Butler,* Little Sisters Bookstore and others defended or would have allowed the production and distribution of *this,* and they defended it as gay male identity—an identity that equals, promotes, encourages, hence *is* violence, cruelty, degradation, exploitation, assertiveness linked with aggression, strength equated with violence, physical power and the right to overpower, intimidation, control of others, lack of mutuality and disrespect, being hurt presented as pleasurable, violating and being violated presented as identity politics, and aggressive, nonconsensual behavior advanced as normal, liberating, and sexually promoted as such. And it is at this point that rape and domestic violence become issues worth caring about. Rape and domestic violence: those things that happen in private—those things that will continue to happen if gay rights activists, academics, and lawyers continue to use privacy, the pornographer's safety net, to fight for gay rights.

SEXUALIZING GAY MALE RAPE THROUGH PORNOGRAPHIC "FANTASY"

One of the arguments advanced against the production and distribution of heterosexual pornography is that it makes men more tolerant of sex as violence, resulting in sexual assault and abuse against women. Pornography then, far from just theory, becomes a practice. As the following brief analysis of the attitudes of and about men who rape men and who are raped by men indicates, the risk of harm resulting from gay male pornography, like the harms that result from heterosexual pornography, is real. This is particularly true given what gender inequality, now sexualized, has come to mean socially and the effect of sex role stereotypes on gay men in particular. Specifically, if we look at what rape is, what it is about, and what it says about male aggression generally, it does not require much to at least infer that any expressive medium that eroticizes male sexuality as dominance, inequality, abuse, and hierarchy might result in physical and psychological harm to others.

By sexualizing masculinity and femininity through pornography, gay men do exactly this by making the feminine/masculine interaction sexy to gay men. Consuming pornography is done sexually, experienced sexually, *as* sexuality, the practices of which are virtually identical to the top-down sexuality of male dominance. It is the sexuality of male dominance that gay male pornography pushes and eroticizes, and the result is male dominance in action, with all the harms, including rape, that flow from it and sustain it.

In his insightful work on gay male rape, for example, Scarce (1997) provides an account of one man, "Darren," who was abducted by two men in the car park outside his gym. The men held a gun to Darren's head and forced him into their van, handcuffed him, and drove him to a house where they proceeded to sexually humiliate, abuse, and ultimately rape him in the basement. His ordeal says much about power, abuse, and the effect of gender once sexualized in his life and in the lives of his attackers. That he continues to survive is miraculous. That he is willing to talk about it in order to assist others shows an inner strength perhaps known only by those who have survived similar abuse. As such, his words deserve repeating, and all gay men would do well to think critically about the tortuous events he describes:

> . . . They walked around and looked at me and told me they were going to uncuff my hands. At this point they both had guns, and one of the guys uncuffed my hands. They told me to pull off my gym shorts and I did. They made me pull my T-shirt back behind my neck. All I had on was gym shoes, socks, and a jock strap. They made me get into different poses and positions for them for a long time. They held the guns on me the whole time . . . They were touching themselves with one hand, masturbating while they were watching me. One of the guys started talking about how he was going to fuck my butt. They put me over a wooden sawhorse and made me lie across it. They pulled my jockstrap off and then tied my hands and legs to it so I was over it. Then they both took turns raping me. That went on for a long, long time, an hour and a half or so.
>
> They seemed angry when they were fucking me because they did it so hard, with so much force. Earlier when they were using [a] switch on me, it was like they were trying to get every piece

of anger or rage they had out on me. The rest of the time they were more sarcastic or condescending, more trying to humiliate or degrade me than angry. (Scarce, 1997:127-132)

Darren's experience is not pornography. But, after reviewing the materials outlined above, it is clear that it could be. From a sex equality perspective, if this description of a rape appeared in a gay male pornography magazine and was sold and used as sexual practice, it would be pornography, particularly as it encourages, by sexualizing, sexual assault. And to the extent that someone uses it and then acts it out, their victims should be taken seriously when they question "the right" of those who produced and published it as gay male pornography/gay male identity/sexuality to do so.

Indeed, if these passages had appeared in the previous section of this chapter, the reader could be forgiven for mistaking Darren's horror for the "pleasure" defended as sexuality and liberation in quite a few of the exhibits defended in the *Little Sisters* trial: a young, attractive, physically fit male is abducted in a car park. His captors, threatening to kill him and laughing at his fear, drive him to their "rape house." They handcuff him, make him perform, and masturbate while watching him. Stripping him naked, they objectify his body, sexualize his fear, and act out their most vivid pornographic fantasies. Handcuffed, the young man is posed on a platform, whipped with switches, then tied to a sawhorse where he is brutally raped and beaten with a paddle. Throughout it all, degraded and ridiculed, he is made to service men who, while simultaneously sexualizing and condemning his sexuality, find validation in the abuse inflicted by real men needing to reaffirm their masculinity through violence, humiliation, and the stripping away of another man's manhood.

Darren's experience, like that of many men who have been raped, says a great deal about the dangers inherent in a society that sexualizes inequality. What his story epitomizes is misogyny gone mad. Feminizing him in order to condemn him and use him as an unequal, while reasserting their own masculinity through the acting out of sexualized violence, these men do sexually what male dominance requires to survive. By degrading Darren and mocking him sexually for going to gyms (for daring to be more masculine than them—a masculinity they in turn eroticize), these men, through violence, dehumanization, and rape, successfully put Darren back in his place. This empowers them as men. Feminizing him, stripping him of his manhood, they, in turn, prop up their own. Their actions typify homophobia and self-hate in action, sexism made sexy.

These conclusions are further supported by the work of those who have detailed the factors that motivate the rapist. In a 1980 study on men who rape men, for example, Groth and Burgess (quoted in McMullen, 1990) outline the following motivating factors for men convicted of raping other men:

- *Conquest and control:* All assaults served as an expression of power and mastery on the part of the offender;
- *Revenge and retaliation:* In some cases of male rape, the offense is activated by the assailant's anger toward his victim and is regarded by him as some form of retaliation;
- *Sadism and degradation:* For some assailants, aggression itself becomes eroticized, and they find excitement in the sexual abuse and degradation of their victim;
- *Conflict and counteraction:* Another component in some male rapes is the assailant's attempt to punish the victim as a way of dealing with his unresolved and conflicting sexual interests. (McMullen, 1990:27)

In the same study, the authors describe the views of one man detailing his attitude toward his victim as follows:

> I had the guy so frightened I could have made him do anything I wanted. I didn't have an erection. I wasn't really interested in sex. I felt powerful, and hurting him excited me. Making him suck me was more to degrade him than for my physical satisfaction. (McMullen, 1990:27)

Similarly, in analyzing the rape of men by men in prisons, Susan Brownmiller (1985) notes that to talk of rape as violence only, without acknowledging the extent to which that violence is gendered, risks overlooking the extent to which the "sex" in the expression "sex crime" is very much socially constructed and enforced by sexism and the homophobic desire for male supremacy. Within the context of gay male pornography, any analysis that omits gender also risks valorizing the violence that we then risk sexualizing and thus normalizing. Brownmiller notes, for example, that prison rape can be seen "as an acting out of power roles within an all male, authoritarian environment in which the weaker, younger inmate . . . is forced to play the role that in the outside world is assigned to women" (1985:258). As MacKinnon (1997) explains:

> this lowers the victim's status, making him inferior as a man by social standards. For a man to be sexually attacked, by placing him in a woman's role, demeans his masculinity; he loses it so to speak. What he loses, he loses through gender, as a man. (1997:10)

To this, one would add only that for a man to sexually attack, by confirming his role as a real man, reaffirms his masculinity. What he maintains or gains, he gains through gender, as a man. Hence, when a man sexually abuses another man, his actions are gender based, thus sexual. Male domination by some men over other men is part of the social system of gender whereby men dominate women and through which straight men dominate gay men. Hence, male rape, like antigay violence generally, is also a weapon of sexism, finding its source in the social institutions that prop up masculinity and, in so doing, suppress any sexual expression that threatens it.

Given these findings, gay men might well want to discourage, rather than sexualize, the harms documented. Unfortunately, gay men are not discouraging them. And so I ask: in examining what gay male pornography is, should we not at least acknowledge that harm is possible given that this medium is intended for men who, as gay men, are socially feminized, are told they are inferior, and, as such, are likely to take quite seriously the message? The message is conveyed in a medium that fuses dominance with sexuality, that promotes male empowerment by dictating that power is to be found in a sexuality in which he who dominates is powerful, and he who does not, is not. Should we not be concerned that gay male pornography represents sexuality generally and it is *this* sexuality, the sexuality of male dominance, that is at the root of all that is antiwoman and antigay, but promale? Gay male pornography encourages this hierarchy, from which harm seems inevitable. Consider, for example, the following images from some of the gay male pornography exhibits defended in *Little Sisters,* some of them in issue in the *Little Sisters* case:

> *In a magazine:* A young office worker, dressed in suit and tie, leaves his office and enters his car. From behind he feels a knife.

In his rear-view mirror he sees two men, both dressed in leather, army boots and studded jackets. He is urinated on, raped orally and anally, but described throughout as enjoying it and anxious for more.

The story reads: "Hands on my waist he rammed, slamming the unlubricated head and the whole dry shaft deep inside me. It hurt like hell. I moaned . . . in agony. It was tearing me apart like a chisel in the crack of a stone. I felt myself splitting into two halves and I could do nothing to stop it and I felt my cock stiffen in response. He was ramming into me now like a man possessed, sliding in and out without attention to my screams of pain. It felt like a goddamned log, bark and all, being slid up my crack. I heard his friend screaming, 'fuck him, fuck the hell out of him' and I loved it." (*Little Sisters* Exhibit 49, 1990:56)

The story ends with the following:

"I still had my wallet and my watch." (This is after they've left.) "They hadn't taken anything but my dignity. My underwear was lost in the weeds—and torn apart anyway, but I dressed myself as best I could. I got in the car and drove home. When I got there I parked in the driveway and walked inside, remembering as I always have, to leave the door to the backseat unlocked." (*Little Sisters* Exhibit 49, 1990:56)

In a magazine: A "slave training manual" teaches the reader the proper etiquette for training a slave over the phone. It reads: "Whenever he phones his Master, the slave should be naked, kneeling and wearing tit clamps. When phoned by his Master, the slave should always immediately drop to his knees and continue the call, looking downwards and with his spare hand behind his back. Alternatively, the slave can be taught that when his Master phones, the slave should always, ring off, strip naked except for tit ring and then phone his Master back from a kneeling position of course. The Master should always stand up when making telephone calls to his slave. A curious fact acknowledged by business psychologists is that standing up while conducting a phone conversation increases the apparent authority of the speaker, particularly if the receiver is not standing up. Conversely, kneeling will increase the apparent servility of the speaker. When one party stands and the other kneels, the Master servant relationship is powerfully enforced." (*Little Sisters* Exhibit 48, 1990:13)

As the activist group Men Against Rape and Pornography explains, what the previous quotations essentially provide is a users' manual on how to get and keep power through sex, through sexuality—a message that, given the level of antigay violence within the community, can only hinder the call for equality:

> Although unrecognized and hidden well within our community, rape is very common. Typically, as with male-female rape, the rape is likely to happen on a date or other situation where the victim and rapist already know each other. One man is at another man's apartment and he is pressured or forced to "have sex." This is rape. . . . One man insists on tying another man to the bedpost and says that he needs to do this in order to really "get off." He saw this done to someone else in a video. This is rape. It is about power, domination, force, and control over another person, which has been sexualized. (Men Against Rape and Pornography, 1993)

Building on this analysis, it is also clear that a number of myths about male rape are enforced through the sex that is pornography. These myths, once sexualized, encourage it and undermine attempts to arrest it. Central in this regard is the myth that "no" means "yes," particularly if it is a gay man who says no, because, according to the myth now made sexy through pornography, gay men actually enjoy rape. For us, according to this stereotype, rape *is* sex, so all sex is consensual and enjoyable. Another myth assumes that men are entitled to sex with their partners, whenever they want, even if their partners don't want to (Scarce, 1997:69-70).

If we look at what gay male pornography says and compare this with how rapists and rape victims are believed and supposed to feel, what we see is that gay male pornography encourages and is a sexuality that promises the gay male the power he so desperately wants but that society has denied him; it is a form of power that very much depends on the violent degradation of someone else. This degradation, sexualized and made real though rape, is what makes pornography sexy and what makes rape a consequence of the materials gay rights advocates would have us defend as nonharmful.

Gay male pornography also teaches the rapist that other men enjoy the violation through which he can seek empowerment—that he will find pleasure in an act of violence committed against another. Rape, normalized though sex, becomes gay sex, and in so doing, ensures that gay sex does little more than prop up the sexual hierarchies that make homophobia and sexism sexy and the cornerstone of inequality on the basis of sex. Finally, gay male pornography, produced by and sold to a community in which sexual violence is common, continues to promote materials that tell those who have been raped that they should enjoy and want this abuse. When rape = sex = gay male identity, equality (both within the gay community and society generally) finds that it has no role.

PORNOGRAPHY AND DOMESTIC VIOLENCE: MALE DOMINANCE NORMALIZED THROUGH SEX

Much of the previous is also relevant to the issue of domestic violence. The statistics speak for themselves. Gay men who batter and abuse their partners have specific ideas about masculinity and what it means to be "male." This is, in part, a reaction to a complete lack of positive gay role models, a homophobic environment in which being gay means being "nonmasculine," and the internalization of social rejection and self-hate. Gay men, growing up in a world with little or no positive reinforcement, are inundated with a value system that equates masculinity (as the determiner of appropriate male behavior) with aggression, control, and frequently violence (Island and Letellier, 1991).

Nowhere is this more evident than in the pornography used by these men. Made sexy, masculinity becomes a turn on. Gay male pornography is comprised of "values" such as strength, power, lack of tenderness, vulnerability of the other, control, and nonmutuality. A reexamination of the masculine ideal held by those men who psychologically abuse, rape, beat, and sometimes kill their partners reveals that their practices and value systems are exactly the same. This means, quite literally, that gay male pornography equals, promotes, and sexualizes *this* view of masculinity—the same view that daily results in gay men abusing and killing the men who love them. Although no research has been conducted to determine if gay men who abuse other gay men use gay male pornography, there is no evidence that they do not. To my mind, the fact that gay male pornography does promote through sex the macho as value means that this message— once interpreted by men who may not fit the desired norm but who are told and feel that they can and should through sex—has the potential to cause considerable harm.

For some gay men, overcompensation for their sense of nonworth becomes inevitable. Applying what they believe will provide control, power, and what they hope will amount to social acceptance, those who ultimately do batter quite literally become the value system they equate with masculinity— something which society thinks is more socially "male," hence appropriate. "As real-live puppets, they perform a role, read a script, and mechanically act-out whatever their ideas are about masculinity" (Island and Letellier, 1991:52). The result, for some, is an effort to be the masculine prototype. These men interpret assertiveness to mean aggression and hence ignore the rights and feelings of others, think of strength as a license to be sexually violent or intimidating, see power as a license to terrorize and view mutuality as a threat to these privileges (1991:52). They follow a prescription, a recipe for masculinity now made sexy and normal through pornography, and, after beating their partners, excuse their behavior by claiming that their actions are sexually acceptable.

Although much of the previous also applies to heterosexual men, the effects of this "masculinity as norm" myth for the gay male already affected by deeply embedded stereotypes are particularly significant. Indeed, one might think that it is only those who already conform to the masculine prototype who beat their partners, but studies reveal quite the opposite. Many gay male domestic batterers do "not fit the stereotypical super-macho man." Rather, they suffer from what can only be termed "failed macho syndrome." Socially rejected for their failure to conform, they feel that they do not reach the masculine ideal of "dominance and coolness" and, in an effort to reach the desired "norm," attempt to control other people, often through sex, in an effort to become that which society has told them they are not (Island and Letellier, 1991:52-53).

These findings say a great deal about the power of systemic homophobia as a social force aimed at limiting same-sex sexual activity. Gay men, to the extent that they threaten to undermine masculine/feminine polarity, are terrorized so as to diffuse this threat. Ridiculed as feminine, defined as socially inferior to "real" men, gay men are silenced so as to ensure that they do not reveal their sexual orientation, and those who do are systematically attacked. Left with few options, the result for many is fear, confusion, and self-hate. They are told that they can reject the masculine norm and be further harassed, or they can attempt to become it (and, in so doing, hide any distinct, nonmisogynistic gay male identity), thus making themselves (as gay) invisible. Unfortunately, the pervasiveness of antigay male violence and discrimination means that many gay men may overcompensate through sex and attempt to adhere to those sexual "values" that they believe will make them less visible, more "male." As Island and Letellier's (1991) findings indicate, this overcompensation can result in some particularly destructive behaviors, causing physical and emotional harm against others. They also ensure that male dominance, now sexualized, hence normalized, remains in place.

CONCLUSION: NO CAUSE FOR CELEBRATION

To date, our community has shown an apparent unwillingness to take seriously the very real harms of intracommunity rape and domestic violence. There are undoubtedly a number of reasons for this. The question I have attempted to pose in this brief discussion is whether, to some extent, our inaction can be explained by the pornography many now defend as central to gay male identity and liberation—pornography which now, because of *Lawrence,* will almost certainly be defended as a right central to gay male liberation.

The facts seem to support this assertion. The materials at issue in *Little Sisters* were defended by many as indicative of what it means to be a gay male today. If this is the case, the only conclusion one can draw is that we have become so obsessed with defending and *becoming* pornography that the most serious of subjects now find themselves sexualized, trivialized, or worse (as in the case of antigay violence)—glorified as a source of sexual empowerment.

For pro-pornography advocates, gay male pornography is harmfree. To these people, I say: materials that encourage a masculinity through which male sexuality is defined as aggression, violence, and degradation of others, when used by men who live in a homophobic society and already feel socially inferior, these materials offer little or no incentive to feel otherwise. Instead, the materials encourage these men to become the very thing that society already tells them they are not, but should be (i.e., more "male," sexually and socially). While disturbing, the consequences of male rape and gay male domestic abuse remain too real and too serious for us to simply ignore. We can not assume that effects of pornography are nonharmful.

In many ways, all I am asking for in this chapter is for gay men to reject the violence endemic in our community, to question its causes, and consider where we go from here. We also need to rethink how best to litigate our right to be free from inequality and harm—harm in all its forms. Gay rights today, exemplified by the *Little Sisters* litigation, inevitably strengthened and made possible by the privacy doctrine now affirmed in *Lawrence,* has come to mean male-dominant rights, the very essence of all that is antigay. Defined by the pornographic sexual exploitation of others, we have now accepted and promoted a model of identity and community that is more concerned with the use and abuse of others than with liberation from sexual hierarchy.

Ultimately, gay men may find that they have at last achieved manhood and the power that comes with being able to do what you want and with whom in private. But at what price? Becoming a man, learning to be one, does nothing for gay male liberation. It ensures only that some of us become more heterosexually acceptable—a liberation tactic devoid of strategy, which is neither radical nor empowering. Privacy, a heterosexual construct, used most successfully in the United States and other countries by pornographers, is not a model of liberation of which any of us can be particularly proud. Sex equality is.

REFERENCES

Brownmiller, Susan (1985). *Against our will: Men, women and rape.* New York: Simon and Schuster.

Calderwood, Deryck (1987). The male rape victim. *Medical Aspects of Human Sexuality,* 53:78-86.

Duncan, David F. (1990). Prevalence of sexual assault victimization among heterosexual and gay/lesbian students. *Psychological Reports,* 66:84.

Dworkin, Andrea (1974). *Women hating.* New York: Plume.

Dworkin, Andrea and Catharine MacKinnon (1988). *Pornography and civil rights: A new day for women's equality.* Minneapolis: Organizing Against Pornography.

Greenhouse, Linda (2003). Justices, 6-3, legalize gay sexual conduct in sweeping reversal. *New York Times,* June 27, <http://www.nytimes.com/2003/06/27/national/27GAYS.html?ex=105768293&ei=1&en=6c14be9ab4122e00>.

Goyer, Peter and Henry Eddelman (1984). Same sex rape of nonincarcerated men. *American Journal of Psychiatry,* 141:576-582.

Hickson, Ford C.I., Davies, Peter M., Hunt, Andrew J., Weatherburn, P., McManus, Thomas J., and Coxon, Anthony P.M. (1994). Gay men as victims of non-consensual Sex. *Archives of Sexual Behavior,* 23(3):281-294.

Island, David and Patrick Letellier (1991). *Men who beat the men who love them.* Binghamton, NY: Harrington Park Press.

MacKinnon, Catharine (1989). *Toward a feminist theory of the state.* Boston: Harvard University Press.

MacKinnon, Catharine (1997). *Brief of National Organization on Male Violence et al in Joseph Oncale v. Sundowner Offshore Services, Inc. et al,* US Supreme Court, No. 96-568, dated August 11.

MacKinnon, Catharine (2001). *Sex equality.* New York: Foundation Press.

McMullen, Richie J. (1990). *Male rape: Breaking the silence on the last taboo.* London: GMP Publishers.

Men against Rape and Pornography (1993). *Looking at gay porn.* Available from MARAP, PO Box 8181 Pittsburgh, PA 15217.

Mezey, Caroline (1992). *Male victims of sexual assault.* London: Oxford University Press.

Pharr, Suzanne (1988), *Homophobia: A weapon of sexism.* Little Rock, AR: Chardon Press.

Scarce, Michael (1997). *Male on male rape: The hidden toll of stigma and shame.* New York: Insight Books.

Stoltenberg, John (1990) You can't fight homophobia and protect the pornographers at the same time—An analysis of what went wrong with *Hardwick.* In Leidholt, D. and Raymond, J. (Eds.), *The sexual liberals and the attack on feminism* (pp. 184-190). New York: Athene Press.

Waterman, Caroline and Lori Dawson (1989). Sexual coercion in gay male relationships: Predicators and implications for support services. *Journal of Sex Research,* 26(1):118-124.

Cases

Lawrence v. Texas, 123 S. Ct. 2472 (2003)

Little Sisters Book and Art Emporium v. Canada (Minister of Justice) (2000), 2 SCR 1120.

R v. Butler, (1992) Supreme Court of Canada, 1 SCR 452 (SCC).

Roe v. Wade, 410 US 113 (1973)

Court Documents

Factum of the Appellant Little Sisters Book and Art Emporium (1999). In the case of *Little Sisters Book and Art Emporium v. Canada (Minister of Justice),* Supreme Court of Canada, Court File No. 26858, dated 19 July.

Factum of the Intervener EGALE (2000). In the case of *Little Sisters Book and Art Emporium v. A.G. Canada,* Supreme Court of Canada, Court File No. 26858.

Factum of the Intervener Women's Legal Education and Action Fund (LEAF) (1991). In *R v. Butler* (SCC), File No. 22191.

Little Sisters Trial Exhibits (1989). Exhibit number 198, *Advocate Men,* December, published by Liberation Publications.

Little Sisters Trial Exhibits (1990). Exhibit 49, *MACII 19: A Drummer Super Publication,* January.

Little Sisters Trial Exhibits (1990). Exhibit 48, *Dungeon Master, No. 39—The Male SM Publication.*

Little Sisters Trial Exhibits (1984). Exhibit number 213, *Juice: True Homosexual Experiences,* Volume 5.

Chapter 9

Queer Men and Sexual Assault: What Being Raped Says About Being a Man

Rus Ervin Funk

I am a bisexual man. I am a social worker and an activist for human rights, with a particular focus on what has been called gender-based violence, and have worked mostly in the United States (with short stints in Canada, Israel, and Palestine). In this chapter, I examine how gay and bisexual men experience and relate to masculinity from the lens of my own experiences as an out bisexual, but also with the grounding of someone who has worked in the area as a professional and an activist for many years.

As someone who has worked with countless men and women who have been sexually victimized, I can attest to the profound impact that sexual assault has on the person who has been victimized. The experience of being sexually assaulted has deep and often long-lasting impacts on people, in ways that they are often unaware of initially. It is only after a period of time that the full effect of a sexual assault (or series of sexual assaults) becomes clear. For men in general, being sexually assaulted often has a tremendous impact on their self-perception as men, the way that they understand themselves as men and masculinity in general, and how they relate to notions of masculinity. For gay and bisexual men, this experience is no less true.

In this short chapter, I provide an overview of sexual assault and provide some insight based on my experiences and a review of the literature about how gay and bisexual men who have been sexually victimized experience masculinity.

Before I begin, a couple of notes are worthy of exploration. First, a note about language. Gay and bisexual men who are sexually victimized are more than their experiences of sexual victimization. As such, I do not refer to them, here, as either "victim" or "survivor." The label "victim" is inherently disempowering language, and I refuse to use that except in the most legalese of trainings or presentations—and even in these situations I resist using this language. The term "survivor" is much more empowering and better reflects the reality as experienced by people who have been victimized—*that they have survived*. Even still, the term "survivor" is a label. Both "victim" and "survivor" become identity markers for people who have been victimized. They become "Rus Funk—the survivor." Rather, I think it important that the person becomes the focus of our attention, not the fact that he or she has been victimized. It is not much different from how we have learned to refer to people living with AIDS. The language shifted from AIDS victims, to AIDS patients, to *people*. For me, particularly in this chapter, the same is true for the men I talk about here who have been victimized. They are *people* who have had this experience. Being victimized is neither an identity nor a role; it is an experience (in some cases, a series of experiences), and that experience does not and should not define them.

A second point is that I am speaking of my experience as a European American in the United States. Although I have worked with men and women from many different backgrounds and cultures who have been victimized, I am still European American. The experiences of racial and cultural privilege that I experience as a result influence how I receive information—including information with gay and bi men who have been victimized. My experience in the United States limits my view to some degree. There are important differences in terms of how masculinity is seen and understood. I cannot speak well to those differences. There are also many similarities (due largely to U.S. cultural imperialism), and it is those similarities that I aim to speak for.

There are also important differences in how sexual assault is understood and defined—both legally and extralegally. Each country and most states within each country have different legal definitions of sexual assault; most cultures also have subtle but profound differences in how sexual assault is defined and understood. These differences are impossible for me to adequately address—due not only to the lack of space, but also to my lack of knowledge about these differences. To the reader, from wherever you are reading, I hope that you will take what you can from my discussion here and make it meaningful for your own self and the country and culture from which you are reading this.

DEFINING SEXUAL ASSAULT

When discussing the issues of gay and bisexual men who have been sexually victimized, it is important that we begin with an exploration of what sexual assault means. The meaning of sexual assault, of course, begins with legal and cultural definitions, but it also includes much more than that. So to begin this section, I offer an overview of legal definitions and victim-centered definitions.

Legal Definitions

The legal definitions vary from state to state (within the United States) and even more broadly across national boundaries. There is no one universally accepted definition of sexual assault. In general, however, sexual assault is a broadly defined term that includes various specific acts (at least legally). These legal definitions place limitations on what is or is not considered as sexual assault, and for many men places their experience outside the legal framework. For example, in most states in the United States and in many other countries, rape is defined as only being the forced penetration of the vagina. By definition, then, this excludes men. Although there are often (at least in the United States) legally defined terms that do include men, often with the same sentencing guidelines as rape, the legal limitations on what is considered rape places it outside the bounds of how men can define their own experience. For many men, what they experienced was a rape, yet the legal definitions do not recognize this self-definition. As a result, many men experience a forced contradiction between their lived reality and what the law defines for them. Many also feel that this discounts their experience.

Feminist Definitions

A feminist definition of sexual assault is "any forced or unwanted sexual contact as defined by the person experiencing the force." This definition recognizes the various forms of force that a person might experience—coercion, manipulation, haranguing, guilting, pressure, threats, intimidation, trickery, lies, etc. In addition, this feminist definition recognizes that the *experience* is what defines it as a rape. The experience is based on the person to whom it happens.

DYNAMICS/STATISTICS/IMPACT

The best community studies find that about 16 percent of males are sexually abused as children (Finkelhor, 1994). Men are perpetrators of about 86 percent of male victimization cases (regardless of the age of the male). The older the male, the greater the probability that the person who abuses him is also male (Whealin, 2000).

Boys are more likely than girls to be sexually victimized by strangers and authority figures (Whealin, 2000). As males grow older, they are more likely than women to be sexually assaulted with more severe forms of physical violence, the use of weapons, or by gangs. As boys grow older, their risk of being sexually victimized decreases, whereas women's risk of being sexually victimized remains relatively stable throughout their lives.

Beyond these statistics and statements, rape is a traumatizing experience that often has far-reaching implications. Who one is sexually (how they define themselves sexually, the kinds of sexual practices they enjoy, who they find attractive, etc.) is perhaps one of the most private aspects of human behavior and identity. Rape is by definition an intrusive act that involves another person (or persons) violating the most private, most sacred parts of another person. Although often focused on the sexual body parts of the person victimized, sexual assault is so much more than a sexual act. It is an extreme act of violence and contempt.

Perhaps some of the most degrading aspects of a rape are not the physical acts but the verbal abuse that is targeted upon the person who is victimized. Men who rape often use extremely violent forms of verbal abuse during the commission of the rape. It is through the verbalizations that the true contemptuousness of the crime gets depicted. In addition, if there is any doubt that rape is a gendered crime, that doubt gets erased when examining the verbal abuse used during the commission of a rape. Men who are raped are often referred to as "bitches," "sluts," "whores," "women," "girls," and other gendered terms that clearly demonstrate how rapists conceive of rape—it is meant as a crime against women, even when men are the targets.

People who are sexually victimized frequently experience a great deal of shame and self-blame for being victimized. They often report feelings that they should have "known better" or that they should have done something differently in order to avoid or prevent the sexual victimization they experienced. They feel to blame for "allowing" themselves to be in a situation where they could have been sexually assaulted. These feelings of self-blame and shame are increased in situations in which the rapist was a friend, colleague, or acquaintance, as well as when the person who was victimized may have experienced some physical bodily reactions to the sexual assault. These feelings are also exacerbated by the verbal abuse heaped on by the rapist. As with most verbal abuse, some aspects of what the rapist says "ring true" to the person who was sexually victimized, and this becomes a trigger for the blame and shame.

For men who are sexually victimized, a sexual assault tends to trigger many of these same issues and feelings, with some differences because of masculinity training. Manhood training teaches men that they should be able to protect themselves (Rogers and Terry, 1984), especially against unwanted sexual contact, and that they are supposed to value sexual contact (Trivelpiece, 1990). Manhood also trains men that they should be able to handle problems on their own and remain stoic and resolute in times of crisis. Most men report that they would "never allow" themselves to be sexually assaulted (based on the myth of the amount of power that people who are victimized have at the time that they are being assaulted in relation to the rapist/s). Hegemonic masculinity is so tied to homophobia, and the myths of male sexual assault are so confused with sexual (and sexualized) ideas, that it is triggered by any discussion that men are raped. So this defensive posturing results—men positioning themselves as something, anything, other than someone who could be sexually victimized: invulnerable, self-reliant, "strong," self-protective, able to defend oneself effectively, powerful, sexually dominant, etc.

The dynamics of sexual assault create a situation in which men are being sexually touched in a way that they may not like or want, but because of men's physiological makeup, their bodies may respond to the touching that they do not like. In other words, men may and often do experience erection and ejaculation while being sexually assaulted. This mixed message of emotionally experiencing the assault as intrusive, violent, and abusive while physiologically responding to being touched in their sexual areas often increases the confusion, guilt, and shame that many men experience. This shame and self-blame is one of the reasons that men have such a low rate of reporting the incident.

QUEER MEN AND SEXUAL ASSAULT

Gay and bisexual men are not very different from heterosexual men in these regards. Although having somewhat of a different relationship with and understanding of hegemonic masculinity, gay and bi men also have often bought into many of the same ideas that are listed previously. When they experience sexual assault, many of the same responses are triggered in gay and bi men as are triggered in heterosexual men. To say, however, that gay and bi men who are sexually assaulted are no different from heterosexual men who are sexually assaulted is too simplistic and does not allow for the variances among gay and bi men and their relationships with masculinity, violence, and their own bodies (which in turn are influenced by their lived experiences of being sexual).

Gay and bisexual men, of course, run the gamut in their relationship to hegemonic masculinity. There are those who position themselves following the line of the most masculine extreme of masculinity and who are, in effect (if not self-identity), "real men" who just happen to have sex with other men. On the other extreme are bi or gay men who position themselves and act in direct opposition to and in resistance of hegemonic masculinity. How a sexual assault impacts on gay or bi men depends, in part, on their particular relationship to hegemonic masculinity but also depends, in part, on the dynamics of the sexual assault.

Gay and bisexual men are sexually assaulted in a number of ways. Gay and bisexual men, like heterosexual men, can be sexually assaulted randomly, with no apparent connection to anything else. Gay and bisexual men are also sexually assaulted as part of a hate crime. This may be gay bashing, but also occur as part of other forms of hate crimes. Gay and bi men of color, for example, may be bashed primarily not for their sexual orientation, but for their color; and a sexual assault in this dynamic may not be directed at his sexual orientation but at his color. Gay and bi men can also be sexually assaulted on dates or as part of an ongoing sexual relationship—akin to "marital rape" in the heterosexual world.

Each of these forms of sexual assault will tend to have different kinds of impacts on the men who are assaulted, and on their relationship to and understanding of masculinity. I will go into these dynamics in more detail below. Before I enter into this dialogue, however, I want to suggest one key point. It is difficult if not impossible for most people to separate their sexual identity from the rest of their identities. When a person experiences a traumatic event, such as a sexual assault, it is grotesquely unfair to expect that person to not experience that trauma as a whole person—including as a sexual person. Thus, gay or bisexual men often experience a sexual assault not only as men, but also as gay or bi (as well as the rest of their identities—Christian, Moslem, or Jew; African American, European American, or Latino; Southerner, New Yorker, or Californian). Depending on where a person is in his coming-out process, and the dynamics of the sexual assault, the impact may strike more or less to the core of his sexual identity. Because of this, and the limits of space, I am going to focus primarily on the experiences of gay and bi men who are sexually assaulted as part of a gay bashing and as part of acquaintance rape. The issues faced by gay or bi men who are sexually assaulted as random violence or who are sexually assaulted as a part of some other form of hate crime as related to masculinity will be addressed through the discussion of these other types of sexual assault.

Rape As Part of Gay Bashing

It is unclear how common it is for gay men to be raped or otherwise sexually victimized during gay-bashing incidents. What is clear is that this threat is ever-present for gay and bisexual men and that many gay-bashing incidents have elements of sexualized violence as part of the violence as it is committed. The sexualized aspects of a gay bashing can include anything from sexualized verbal abuse, to groping, to rape.

Acquaintance Rape in Men's Relationships with Men

More common than sexual assaults during gay bashing are the sexual assaults that queer men experience in their dating relationships with other men. Although rare, there is no reason to believe that "date rape" is any less common in gay male dating than it is in heterosexual dating. Kalichman and Rompa (1994), for example, found that 29 percent of gay and bisexual men in a large midwestern U.S. city experienced sexual coercion (see also Kalichman et al., 2001). As with heterosexual date rape, the actual behavior that occurs includes a variety of behaviors. The common factor is some form of unwanted or forced sexual contact.

Response of Queer Men to the Rape of Queer Men

Gay and bi men are sexually victimized in a context. Often that context includes, in part, the community that they define themselves as being a part of, and the larger queer men's community in general. Most queer men know that they are part of a special club—one that is in the minority, but that exists nearly everywhere. Most of us can go into nearly any town and know how to find out where to go to meet other queer men—for a host of reasons not the least of which is camaraderie.

As a result of being part of a community with tentacles that reach into nearly every corner of any society, one would assume that when men are sexually victimized, or in any way traumatized, an immediate support network would be available for that man. Tragically, that is far from the case.

Although there does seem to be some room for men to discuss their experiences and obtain support from certain aspects of the queer community when discussing being raped as part of a gay bashing, these resources are, in fact, limited and "ghettoized." Men who are raped by a date or spouse often not only do not receive support from within the community, but often are explicitly told to not talk about the incident or are threatened with being removed from the community. The queer male community seems both extremely reticent to discuss the issues and all but unwilling to offer supports to gay and bi men who are sexually assaulted.

"Marshall" provides an excellent example of this. Marshall was a twenty-eight-year-old African-American man who lived in a larger northeastern city that also had a large and thriving gay community. Marshall had recently moved to this city when he began dating

"Mark," a man he had met at a dance club. They went out on two or three dates when Marshall agreed to go away for the weekend together. During this weekend trip, Mark raped Marshall twice. Although Marshall did agree to go on the trip with Mark, and did engage in some sexual play with Mark, both times Marshall explicitly stated that he did not want to engage in anal sex with Mark. Mark refused to listen and respect Marshall, and committed the rapes.

Upon returning to their community, Marshall sought support from the queer community through both formal resources and informal supports. He called the local gay men's health clinic, the gay community center, the gay hotline, as well as the local antiviolence project (a program working to address gay bashing). Although many of these services did attempt to offer support, they clearly were not prepared to respond to Marshall's needs, and his experience included a great deal of victim blaming. At nearly every turn, he was asked why he agreed to go on the trip with someone he knew for such a short time and was asked how clear he was about saying "no" to Mark in regard to the anal sex. He was also asked, repeatedly, why he stayed with Mark for the rest of the trip after the first sexual assault. All of these questions have unstated presumptions about his experience and shift responsibility for the rapes away from Mark and onto Marshall.

Marshall's experiences informally were even worse. Because he was new to the community, many of the friends he had were also friends of Mark. Undoubtedly, these friends felt torn, once Marshall demonstrated the courage and began to talk with them about what he had experienced. But their being torn turned into behavior that not only further isolated Marshall, but which suggested to him that he not talk about it and that his continued attempts to talk about his experiences threatened the gay community as a whole—as if by talking about his experience, the gay community in that town would collapse in on itself, or be subject to increased scrutiny and worse. Again, blame was placed not on Mark's rape of Marshall, but on Marshall for having the audacity to try and talk about it.

If the queer men's community is not prepared to respond supportively to queer men who are sexually assaulted, then we leave them to their own devices to manage the healing process. Part of their healing is struggling with what their being sexually assaulted means to them as men and to their relationship with and understanding of masculinity. We also, as a community, fail to address the issues of what sexual assault means to us, collectively, as queer *men*.

SEXUAL ASSAULT AND QUEER MALE IDENTITY

Imbedded in the assault experiences and the healing process for queer men is their experience of the assault on them as sexual beings, as queer, but also as *men*. The experience of the assault has effects on how queer men see themselves, as well as the impact of their community and the kinds of support they are offered and receive.

As described previously, the two main contexts in which queer men are sexually assaulted are on dates and during gay-bashing assaults. These two different contexts for sexual assault have a different impact on how queer men experience the assaults, *as men*, as well as their experience of their healing process.

Traditional manhood training in many cultures teaches men to be aggressive (up to and including using violence), self-directive, assertive, self-assured, protective, risk taking, and self-reliant (see Connell, 1995, 2001; Whitehead & Barrett, 2001), among other qualities. As discussed elsewhere in this book, queer men have tumultuous and complex relationship with traditional masculinities. In some ways, queer men seem to achieve these qualities to the same degree as heterosexual men. In other ways, however, queer men are seen as other than masculine based on defining (or being defined) as queer. In other words, there are ways that queer men are still *men* and still strive to achieve the markers of manhood within their culture; while in other ways, queer men seek other definitions of manhood within a queer context; and still other ways, queer men may reject the notion of manhood altogether. Being sexually assaulted adds yet another complication to this already convoluted relationship between queer men and masculinity.

As Susan Griffin (1979) notes, "male eroticism is wedded to power" (p. 188). By this she suggests that part of male training in relation to experiencing erotic feelings is based on our being in control of erotic experiences. Put another way, [heterosexual] men define the boundaries of sexual relating and initiate most sexual encounters. Men get off by being on top as much as by the erotic, emotional, and physical contact.

Because most queer men learn the lessons of masculinity before they begin exploring their sexual or affectional feelings for other men, this dynamic is not foreign. Many queer men struggle with the ways that power and control get entangled in their sexual and erotic feelings for and relationships with other men. Being sexual and affectionate with another man challenges the ideas and ideals of male eroticism in a heterosexist climate. Our experience of sex and erotic connection with other men (or for bisexual men, with other men and/or women) is based on our experience of and relation to the power that we have and need in those relationships. How that power is experienced depends, of course, on the individual and his relationships. Being a top, a bottom, or someone who prefers sex side-by-side involves, to some degree, the ways that queer men attempt to grapple with this dynamic.

Sexual assault, as discussed previously, is also about power—and places men who are raped in perhaps *the* most vulnerable position in relation to sexual power. A sexual assault directly attacks one's sexuality, as well as what it means to be a man. By definition, being raped means being powerless in a sexual situation. For most men, queer or het, this is an extremely foreign experience. Because of the way that manhood is connected to being powerful (or at least not powerless) in sexual experiences, a rape is often experienced as an assault against one's manhood. As "John" a nineteen-year-old gay man living in Washington, DC, put it, "But men aren't supposed to be raped!" Putting aside for a moment that this statement suggests that women *are* supposed to be raped, this statement exposes the dilemma that many men, queer and het, face who have been sexually assaulted. Rape is understood (although frequently denied) as a gendered crime: rape is something that men do, and that women have done to them. A man who is raped, then is, at least momentarily, not a man. Because a queer man's masculinity is already suspect—even to himself—being sexually assaulted can exaggerate this questioning of his masculinity to himself and certainly to others. This presumed questioning by others of his masculinity for being both queer and now a rape victim-survivor is often internalized in his efforts to deal with and respond to his experience of being raped. His *experience* is that the rape and the healing process is a threat to his already questionable masculinity.

To further compound queer men's experiences of being raped, our bodies are made to respond to stimulation. When I know chocolate is around, I begin to salivate and become very distracted. This dynamic is one of the wonders of being human; we experience our reality and the various subtleties of our experiences *in* our bodies. Being raped is experienced in a man's body. Part of what can be confusing for men, however, is that their bodies may respond in ways that betray the experience of the rape—their bodies may respond to the touch. Queer men can and do experience erection and ejaculation during sexual assaults. This in no way suggests that queer men enjoy some aspects of being raped. Many queer men, however, experience their body's response as evidence that they "must have" experienced some pleasure in the assault.

But queer men's experiences of being sexually assaulted and the crisis of masculinity that arises as a result, do not end once the rape is completed. Not only is the healing process rife with potholes that raise the question of queer men's masculinity, but the response of their community(ies) also proves problematic for queer men as they heal.

As described previously, hegemonic masculinity—including hegemonic queer masculinity—suggests that men should be self-sufficient and self-reliant. With the advent of HIV/AIDS, queer men have become more amenable to asking for help and support, but we still are far from adept at asking for help when we need it. Experiencing a sexual assault and the healing process from such an assault often requires that queer men ask for help—from help lines and support centers, from police, from prosecuting attorneys, from advocacy agencies . . . The process of healing is rarely done alone. Yet masculinity demands that we "handle it" (whatever the "it" may be). Asking for help, even for queer men, is often experienced as demeaning. This "demeaningness" of asking for help is essentially tied to our views of ourselves as "men."

The process of healing, which often includes asking for support, means interacting with various parts of the community that may not be supportive, and may in fact be downright hostile, to us as queer men who have survived sexual assault. As Marshall's experience describes, queer men often face less than receptive and supportive responses when they come out as having been sexually assaulted within the "family." Queer men also often face less than supportive, ignorant, and/or openly hostile responses from mainstream (i.e., heterosexual) victim's organizations, the police, and prosecuting attorneys.

Because of a severe lack of training and sensitivity, these organizations are not only ill prepared to respond to men who have been victimized; they are often poorly equipped to provide the support and advocacy the queer men need and deserve. In addition, while heterosexual men may face difficulties in these situations due to lack of experience or training, queer men must also face the hostilities of homophobic attitudes and behaviors of the workers. These dynamics also forces queer men to examine their masculinity. Not only are they often in a position of needing to ask for help about an experience that is inherently embarrassing, shameful, and humiliating, but queer men are also often forced to advocate for themselves within this same context. Although hegemonic masculinity certainly has an image and role of fighting for what is right, a role for self-advocacy is not as clear. According to this imagery, "men" advocate for others, but not for themselves. We simply get (by force if need be) what we want. But the experience of healing from sexual assault and meandering through the healing and judicial processes often require that we develop skills in self-advocacy—which, in turn, requires yet another adjustment to our view of ourselves as queer "men."

WHERE WE GO FROM HERE . . .

Clearly much work remains to be done on behalf of queer men who have been raped. Within the "family," we need to do a better job of educating ourselves about the issues of sexual assault and better prepare ourselves for when queer men within our communities come out to us as having been sexually victimized. This means that within our HIV/AIDS service organizations, antiviolence groups, hotlines, community centers, the Metropolitan Community Church, and other local community-based queer organizations, there needs to be a commitment to develop expertise in this area and put ourselves out as ready to support queer men who have been sexually victimized.

Does this mean that we demonize queer men who have been accused of sexual assault or rape? Certainly not. This is part of our work as well: to figure out how to support and advocate for queer men who are victimized, and continue to reach out and hold accountable (the key word here being *hold*) queer men who sexually offend. I consider myself first and foremost an advocate and activist for people who have been sexually victimized. Still, I would much rather see the queer community providing the intervention necessary for queer men who have sexually assaulted; the community needs to take responsibility and be accountable for these actions, rather than leave them to the straight-based organizations and response systems.

It also means that we need to advocate more forcefully with the mainstream organizations to be able to respond to queer men who have been sexually assaulted. Rape crisis centers, in general, have done an enormous amount of work in the area and have been the first to identify, respond to, and reach out to queer men who have been raped. There is a need to continue the work by partnering with them, increasing the capacity to care and expanding the outreach; in particular, there is a need to reach queer men of color and immigrant queer men.

The police and prosecuting offices need to improve their skills and sensitivity, and there is a constant need for queer men to advocate for improved legislation that reflects the issues faced by queer men. As a queer community, we are obligated to work to address these issues and improve our collective, community response to these issues.

Finally, as this chapter (and the lack of references cited) suggests, the need is great for further research to better understand queer men's experiences of being sexually assaulted and their healing process. I found *no* studies to date that specifically looked at what seems to be a fundamental question—How does the experience of being raped affect your view of yourself as a man? If we don't ask the basic questions, how will we ever come up with the answers?

CONCLUDING THOUGHTS

In this short essay, I have attempted to provide an overview of the issues faced by queer men who have been sexually assaulted, specifically related to their understanding of and relationship with themselves as men. This entire text provides a badly needed service to explore queer men's relationships with masculinity; and this chapter was meant to examine one particular aspect of that. Clearly, as is described throughout the chapters in this collection, queer men's relationship with masculinity is a complicated and convoluted one. To suggest, then, that the experience of being raped will have *an* impact on this relationship is ludicrous. This chapter aimed to highlight some of the areas of concern and the issues that seem to commonly arise for queer men who have been raped. More work needs to be done.

A fundamental, but often undefined, human right is the right to be free from violence, including sexual violence. Working for social justice and the expansion of human rights, including sexual rights, means working not only to end sexual violence, but also to provide the kind and quality of services and support that queer men so rightly deserve. I'm not advocating for special rights, just basic rights.

REFERENCES

Connell, R.W. (1995). *Masculinities*. Berkeley: University of California Press.

Connell, R.W. (2001). The social organization of masculinity. In S.M. Whitehead and F.J. Barret (Eds.), *The masculinities reader* (pp. 30-51). Malden, MA: Blackwell Publishers Ltd.

Finkelhor, D. (1994). Current information on the scope and nature of child sexual abuse. *Child Abuse and Neglect* 4:31-53.

Griffin, S. (1979). *Rape: The power of consciousness*. San Francisco, CA: Harper and Row Publishers.

Kalichman, S.C., Benotsch, E., Rompa, D., Gore-Felton, C., Austin, J., Luke, W., Difonzo, K., Buckles, J., Kyomugisha, F., and Simpson, D. (2001). Unwanted sexual experiences and sexual risks in gay and bisexual men: Associations among revictimzation, substance use and psychiatric symptoms. *Journal of Sex Research,* 38(1):147-169.

Kalichman, S.C. and Rompa, D. (1994). Sexual coerced and noncoerced gay and bisexual men: Factors relevant to risk for human immunodeficiency virus (HIV) infection. *The Journal of Sex Research* 32:45-50.

Rogers, C.M. and Terry, T. (1984). Climican intervention with boy victims of sexual abuse. In I. Stuart and J. Greer (Eds.), *Victims of sexual aggression* (pp. 65-85). New York: Van Nostrand Rheinhold Co.

Trivelpiece, J.W. (1990). Adjusting the frame: Cinematic treatment of sexual abuse and rape of men and boys. In M. Hunter (Ed.), *The sexually abused male* (pp. 377-411). New York: Lexington Books.

Whealin, J.M. (2000). Men and sexual trauma: A National Center for PTSD fact sheet. Available from www.ncptsd.org, downloaded on 12/1/2003.

Whitehead, S.M. and Barrett, F.J. (2001). The sociology of masculinity. In S.M. Whitehead and F.J. Barret (Eds), *The masculinities reader* (pp. 1-29). Malden, MA: Blackwell Publishers Ltd.

Chapter 10

HE and $i \neq$ US

Peter Shuttlewood

HE and *i*. *i* and **HE**. **HE** has a name but *i* won't use it here. The memories are still too painful. It is a love which dare not speak its name. **HE** would not like to know that *i* am writing this. **HE** would not approve. *i* do not care. Well, actually, yes *i* do. Therein lies the problem. **HE** doesn't. But *i* do.

Or so the legend goes . . .

- Ancient Romanian vampiric folklore states that in order for a vampire to enter your house he must first be invited.
- Once invited in, he will either:
    —begin the ritual of turning you into a vampire too, or
    —he will suck you dry of all life and leave you as nothing more than an empty shattered shell.

Modern faggot folklore works in much the same way.

HE:
says he's not a poofter, yet
considers me a fuckbuddy
never hits me, unless *i* deserved it, but
likes rough sex
is always on top
won't use a condom
never says **HE** loves me
never shows affection, in case he lets his guard down
can be extremely kind when the mood takes him, but
is a complete and utter bastard when it doesn't

i:
met him the first night I went out to a gay bar, and
was a still a virgin
fell in love straight away
believe he'll change
lied to my mother (ijustfelldownthegoddamstairsmum)
about the black eye and broken arm, which
i probably deserved for using all the hot water
enjoy being the *fuckee* rather than the *fucker,* and
don't consider it rape—even if it is
left once for two weeks, but came back because
he threatened to kill me.

Gay Men's Domestic Violence Is

any
unwanted
physical force
psychological abuse
material or property destruction
inflicted by one man
on another

HOW IT STARTS

"He was nothing special to look at. I was very nervous. It was the first time I'd been out to a gay club. I was a virgin. I knew no other gay men. I had just turned 20 and was sick of being alone and stressing about being gay. I was horny. So I plucked up the courage and went out hoping to meet Mr. Right.

I got drunk quickly on cheap scotch. Trying to steady my shaking hands, I hit the dance floor, hoping the throbbing rhythms would help me relax. I noticed him watching me while I danced. He smiled at me and I smiled back nervously. When I came off the dance floor he came over and started to chat me up.

It made me feel better. He cheered me up and he seemed like a really nice guy. He started buying me drinks. I was getting very drunk. He started kissing me and feeling me up. I got very turned on by this, giving in quickly to his advances. He took me home to his place and we had really hot sex. I let him fuck me. It hurt a little bit but then it felt really, really good. We didn't use a condom. I thought it was all okay. I was too naive to think otherwise. He was more experienced and I let him take control.

Within weeks we were living together. Everything was going well and I was head over heels in love with him. I thought I'd been lucky and found my Mr. Right. Then one day he came home from work really pissed off. He'd had a really bad day and I was trying to cheer him up.

One minute we were having a laugh and joke about his day, and the next minute I was in the bathroom mopping up the blood pouring from my nose. I asked him why he did it, but he didn't want to talk about it. I guess I should have been angry but he was so sad that I felt sorry for him. We ended up going into the bedroom and having sex.

After that, every time he had a bad day or was angry about something, he'd take it out on me. He'd say how useless I was and that he hated me. Then, afterward, while I mopped up my blood or was crouching in a corner crying, he'd say how sorry he was. Then he'd come over to me and hug me and try to kiss it better or start crying himself. Often, we'd end up back in the bedroom having sex.

Over time the violence started to escalate and the begging forgiveness started to fade. Sometimes people would ask about the bruises, but I kept my body covered most of the time so no one could see. After I had to go to hospital the first time, to get stitches in my forehead where he'd hit me with the frying pan, I thought of leaving him and said as much to him. He told me that if I did that he would find me and kill me or out me to my employer and family. I believed him and so was afraid to leave.

I still loved him dearly and hoped that things would get better. Perhaps if I tried to be a better partner and do more for him. I hadn't had a relationship before, so I thought that I had to be doing something wrong. It must be my fault that he was acting this way. It wasn't until much later that I realized that it was he who had a problem—not me."

HOSPITAL RECORDS SHOW:

Black eyes
broken arm
three cracked ribs
burn marks—coffee, an iron, cigarettes
split lips

broken nose
bruising on back and bum from belt buckle welts
two chipped teeth
broken jaw
three stitches in forehead

several more in chest from stab wound
anal tearing
bruised balls
five stitches in back of head
90 stitches in lacerated face

IT'S MY FAULT

SOMETIMES I NEED TO BE HIT. sometimes i even like it. DURING SEX. i can be a bad boy. the odd slap puts me in my place. REMINDS ME. mum hit me when i was bad. IT MUST BE MY FAULT. i must be doing something wrong. otherwise he wouldn't have to hit me. I DESERVE IT.

I DON'T TELL ANYONE. i make up stories. i wear long-sleeve shirts so no one can see the marks on my arms. I LIE A LOT. people must think i'm very clumsy, always falling down stairs or banging into doors or burning myself. IT WAS JUST AN ACCIDENT. i can't tell anyone the truth. it's taboo. NO ONE WOULD BELIEVE ME. i'm bigger and stronger than him. but i would never hurt him.

i know things will get better. HE WILL CHANGE. i stay because i love him. I CAN MAKE HIM CHANGE. i know i can.

ESCAPE

"After nearly a year of being bruised and beaten every day, sometimes two or three times a day, I knew I had to try to escape. I had to get out. But I didn't know how. I was very afraid on him. Afraid that he might kill me. Then luck came my way. Not good luck per se, but luck none the less.

We were in a nightclub and he started ranting at me, accusing me of trying to cruise some guy there. We got into a terrible row which ended with him smashing a glass in my face. I fell to the floor and a crowd gathered around us. This burly security guy came over and grabbed him while someone else called the cops.

I'd always been afraid to go to the police because I was gay and pretty well completely closeted and the cops had a reputation for not believing gays. I had been afraid of being ridiculed. After all, I was bigger and stronger and could have defended myself. Should have defended myself, I suppose.

So anyway, an ambulance came and while I was rushed to hospital to have my face stitched back together again with about eighty or ninety stitches, he was arrested and taken to the watchhouse.

Because I was unconscious the nurses had to remove my blood-stained clothes for me. It was then that they discovered some of the other bruises and cuts. Due to the extent of the injuries I had to stay in hospital for several days. During my stay they gave me an AIDS test. Thankfully it was negative. The doctor convinced me to contact my parents.

When they came to visit I finally summoned the strength to tell them everything. About being gay, about him, about the beatings, everything. Although they were surprised and I suppose more than a little shocked, they didn't show it. They just were concerned for my safety and well-being. Just like parents should be. My dad arranged for me to talk to a solicitor and finally, after a lot of persuading, I agreed to press charges.

We obtained the first of many restraining orders against him. Unfortunately the police decided to let him out of jail on bail with the condition that he didn't break the order. Which of course was the first thing he did.

I moved back into my parents' house, leaving most of what I had at his place. I was too scared to go there then. Afraid he might try to kill me or something. Or maybe even try to hurt my parents. Finally about a month or so later he found out where I was and came around and tried to kick down the door to my parents' house.

He broke the restraining order four or five times, and even though my solicitor contacted the police, he was never imprisoned. Finally one day my I got the courage to go to his house with my dad when I knew he wouldn't be there and we got my stuff. What was left of it anyway. Most of my clothes had been cut up and left strewn about the spare bedroom. Some of my CDs were smashed. I didn't really care. I was free.

He must have finally realized it was over when he saw the stuff gone and the key left on his kitchen table with a one-word note—GOODBYE—because after that he never contacted me again and I was able to start to get on with rebuilding my life. If I hadn't got out when I did I don't know what might have happened."

Now **HE** and *i* ≠ **US**. Now there is a permanent restraining order and a possible jail sentence. But *i* hopefully won't be forced to press any further charges. *i* am still afraid that I might run into him in a club or somewhere, but that is starting to fade. Slowly. Especially now that *i* have met someone new. Who really cares about me. Who loves me as much as *i* love him.

His name is Michael.
And I am no longer *i*.
Now I am **ME!**

Chapter 11

Reading Racial Gaze:
Western Gay Society and Pornographic
Depictions of Asian Men

Simon Obendorf

Gay society [in the West] . . . organized and commercial, is framed around the young middle-class white male. He is its customer and its product. Blacks, Asians and Latin-Americans are the oysters in this meat market. At best we're a quaint specialty for exotic tastes. (Fung, 1996, cited in Tsang, 1996:159)

Each specifically victimized and vulnerable group of women, each tabooed target group—Black women, Asian women, Latin women, Jewish women, pregnant women, disabled women, retarded women, poor women, old women, fat women, women in women's jobs, prostitutes, little girls—distinguishes pornographers genres and subthemes, classified according to customer's favorite degradation. (MacKinnon, 1989:138)

INTRODUCTION

First, an admission, by way of conscious self-incrimination: It was in 1996 that I first wrote to a pornographic video distributorship in the Australian national capital, Canberra, requesting a listing of gay male

I extend my thanks to Sheila Jeffreys and Phillip Darby, whose graduate seminars first challenged me to explore these ideas and provided the space where they were first rehearsed.

pornographic video titles with "Asian" or "Oriental" themes or actors. So, from the outset, I implicate myself in the purchase, circulation, and consumption of gay male pornography—and call into question the connection between my erotic and academic interests in the material I introduce here. The listing of pornographic video titles (which arrived promptly in my mailbox, presumably in anticipation of a quick sale), and indeed its very existence, revealed to me the availability of a wide range of video titles specifically targeted to a Western gay male audience with an interest in viewing pornographic images of Asian men engaged in explicit homosexual activities, both with other Asian men and, more commonly, with male Caucasians. Today, of course, one does not have to wait for a catalog to arrive through the post. Services of this kind are available on the Internet via professionally designed World Wide Web sites where one can not only access and comprehensively search video listings, but also preview and order such pornographic materials for immediate dispatch. Glossy magazines, with titles such as *OG: Oriental Guys,* further exploit this market by presenting soft pornographic photographic images together with erotic cartoons and pornographic fiction featuring Asian men—usually singly or, less commonly, with other Asian men.

This chapter seeks to explore the phenomenon of such Asian-themed gay male pornography—specifically print, photographic, and cinematic/video—in Western gay male culture and society. The majority of pornography circulating within the global gay community emerges from Western countries, due to comparatively liberal publications and censorship laws. Some pornographic materials, though, are produced in Asia itself, and these are being aggressively marketed to a Western audience. An example of this is *The Dove Coos* series of pornographic short stories taken from the pages of Thai gay magazines and translated into English for Western readers—"the dove coos" being a Thai euphemism for penile erection (Allyn, 1992; Jonathan, 1994). Japanese and Thai pornographic videos, commonly of an amateur quality, are also freely circulating within the global economy. Although these Asian-produced forms of pornography may be racially unmarked (in that the figure of the Westerner is rarely or never present), they still circulate and are consumed within Western erotic cultures. Internet pornography is also a growing phenomenon, and the crossovers and similarities between pornography available via the Internet and that sold through traditional distribution channels are considerable. Often, images or video originally published in pornographic magazines or video cassettes/DVDs will be repackaged and distributed (both licitly and illicitly) via the medium of the Internet. Thus, although I have chosen not to emphasize materials drawn from the Internet in much of my analysis, one must remain aware of the extent to which the Internet and new computer technologies function to distribute and reproduce pornographic materials.

I take as my theoretical starting point two discourses which, to date, have shared remarkably little common ground: radical feminism and postcolonial studies. Radical feminism is, perhaps, an obvious framework through which to critically explore pornography. Drawing on the pioneering work of feminist theorists of pornography such as Andrea Dworkin and Catharine MacKinnon (1988), radical feminism can provide many insights to the imperatives operating within contemporary gay male society that lead to the existence of pornography, and which may explain its contents. Yet radical feminism has had a far more complex and turbulent relationship with issues of race and ethnicity. Radical feminists have argued strongly that "a feminist must insist the sex/gender system is the fundamental cause of women's oppression" (Tong, 1998:46), a view that has seen the radical feminist movement censured for its perceived essentialism and indifference to issues of class, race, religion, or ethnicity (Rudy, 2001).

While race has often been written out of radical feminist narratives, issues of ethnicity, culture, and race have been at the core of postcolonialism's critical engagement with issues born from the encounter between the West and its Other (Gandhi, 1998:18-22). Postcolonial studies are concerned with the analysis of relations of dominance and resistance as they were played out during, and have endured in the aftermath of, the experience of Western colonialism. Through the rejection of simplistic and oppositional approaches to understanding historical and contemporary international, intercultural, and intercivilizational processes, postcolonial theory seeks to open up a space of analysis and debate in which the effects and legacies of the colonial encounter can be evaluated and understood. Furthermore, it aims to dismantle colonialist understandings that render the non-West, and non-Western voices, discourses, and experiences, as both foreign and fundamentally inferior (Darby, 1997:8-9). Postcolonial analysis is necessarily historically based, seeing the current position of many non-Western states, cultures, and societies as being shaped in no small part by their particular experiences of colonialism (Darby, 1997). Through postcolonial analysis of these processes, neocolonial relations as they occur within the contemporary world can be identified and strategies of resistance developed (Bhabha, 1994:6). Many feminists, however, have remained skeptical of the transformatory potential of postcolonial forms of analysis. Kay Hymowitz (2003) has argued:

> Postcolonialists . . . have their own binary system, somewhat at odds with gender feminism—not to mention with women's rights. It is not men who are the sinners; it is the West. It is not women who are victimized innocents; it is the people who suffered under Western colonialism, or the descendants of those people, to be more exact.

Although it is fair to say that radical feminism and postcolonialism have remained at arms length from each other, I would suggest that they do share some similarities, and further, that there may be significant intellectual dividends to be earned from bringing them into debate. Both postcolonialism and radical feminism share a commitment to radical change: to question and challenge established orthodoxies such as (respectively) heteropatriarchal and colonial structures of dominance. Furthermore, although there have been significant differences of opinion and of approach, both discourses have taken seriously the feminist doctrine that the personal is political, and both discourses have sought to engage with issues surrounding gender and sexuality. Although many within both schools of thought would argue for the two discourses to maintain a critical distance from each other, I would argue that this should not lead to mutual ignorance or misunderstandings but rather to a sense of productive and respectful dialogue (Darby et al., 2003). It is in such a spirit that I hope this chapter will be read and debated.

I begin by orienting the chapter with a necessarily brief exposition of feminist theorizing on pornography, before moving on to analyze Asian-themed gay male pornography and to apply feminist and postcolonial approaches to such materials. I conclude by arguing that a more politically complete understanding of the nature of Western gay male pornography featuring Asian men can be reached by utilizing feminist antipornography theories coupled with insights drawn from postcolonial forms of analysis.

Any Western Caucasian male scholar must be aware of what Linda Alcoff (1991-1992) has described as the problem of speaking for others—especially the impossibility of ever completely transcending the privileges of membership in the dominant ethnic and gender groups of a racist and sexist society. By utilizing feminist materials in order to undertake this analysis, I in no way mean to silence either women's voices or those of Asian commentators on such materials. In fact, I have tried throughout to bring together many of these voices and allow them space to speak for themselves. I cannot claim to be a disinterested or innocent party to these proceedings, yet I am mindful of Peter Jackson's challenge for

> gay Caucasian writers, artists and academics to move toward the production of images and discursive representations of Asian homosexual men that are based more on identification than either the overvaluation of fetishistic projection or the undervaluation of racist negation. (2000:188)

It is my hope that this chapter can simultaneously demonstrate the continued utility and importance of feminist analyses to gay male culture and also contribute to the diversity of critical opinion already existing and yet to be developed regarding depictions of Asian men in Western gay male pornography.

PORNOGRAPHY: AN OVERVIEW OF RADICAL FEMINIST ANTIPORNOGRAPHIC ANALYSIS

Feminist analyses of pornography grew as a result of the hugely increased availability of pornographic materials following the sexual revolution of the 1960s and 1970s. Jeffreys explains this process:

> [F]or the first time [women] had at their disposal, a panoramic view of what constituted male sexuality . . . The first London anti-pornography group was formed in 1977 because we saw double-page spreads of women's genitals . . . in shop windows and being perused by young boys in corner newsagents shops. We decided we needed to study pornography, to see exactly

what was in it and understand what it told us about men's attitudes to women, about male sexuality and about the construction of heterosexuality. (1990:251)

Many of the central concerns of these radical feminist debates on pornography can be seen in the analyses undertaken on the definition of pornography. In feminist antipornography readings, subordination and power differences, maintained, exploited, fetishized, and presented for the male gaze, constitute pornography's defining features. In their Model Antipornography Civil Rights Ordinance, introduced into the Judiciary Committee of the Commonwealth of Massachusetts in 1992, two of the foremost feminist antipornography campaigners, Andrea Dworkin and Catharine A. MacKinnon (1988), defined pornography thus:

"[P]ornography" means the graphic sexually explicit subordination of women through pictures or words that also includes one or more of the following:

1. women are presented as dehumanized as sexual objects, things or commodities; or
2. women are presented as sexual objects who enjoy humiliation or pain; or
3. women are presented as sexual objects experiencing sexual pleasure in rape, incest, or other sexual assault; or
4. women are presented as sexual objects tied up or cut up or mutilated or bruised or physically hurt; or
5. women are presented in postures or positions of sexual submission, servility, or display; or
6. women's body parts—including, but not limited to, breasts or buttocks—are exhibited such that women are reduce to those parts; or
7. women are presented being penetrated by objects or animals; or
8. women are presented in scenarios of degradation, humiliation, injury, torture, shown as filthy or inferior, bleeding, bruised or hurt in a context that makes these conditions sexual.

The use of men, children, or transsexuals in the place of women in this definition is also pornography for purposes of this law. (1988:138-139)

Under such a definition, which covers both women and men, pornography is seen to be a tool to perpetuate and validate male dominance, and to objectify, degrade and dehumanize its subjects (Dworkin, 1988). This is not an analysis solely from within the feminist movement. In the 1972 collection *The Case Against Pornography*, Robert Stoller argued that in pornography "[t]here is always a victim, no matter how disguised: no victim no pornography" (1972:111). Yet Stoller goes on to use this fact to reaffirm hetero-patriarchal dominance by condemning the use of pornography as perversion, defining such perversion as "indefinitely repeating conscious preference for a genitally stimulating exciting act which is not heterosexual intercourse" (1972:111). Antipornographic discourse, in this case, is utilized not to protect women from being pornographic subjects or objects of the male gaze, but to reaffirm their place within the heterosexual milieu.

Furthermore, by reaffirming male dominance, and by constructing the pornographic subject as an object of hate, of filthiness, of degradation, and of sexual availability, pornography legitimates and reinforces the desires and preeminence of members of the (hetero)patriarchal elite within society. As Dworkin states, "[p]ornography is not made up of old white men. It isn't . . . They are doing this to us [women]; or protecting those who do this to us" (1997:133). Catharine MacKinnon writes:

> It [pornography] connects the centrality of visual objectification to both male sexual arousal and male models of knowledge and verification, objectivity with objectification. It shows how men see the world, how in seeing it, they access and possess it, and how this is an act of dominance over it. (1989:138)

By identifying the masculinist ideology of dominance which is so much pornography's raison d'être, feminist antipornography theorists have also identified the trend, identified by MacKinnon and Dworkin in their Antipornography Ordinance, of treating pornographic subjects, and by corollary, all members of the groups from which they originate, as merely sexually available bodily parts, subservient "holes" willing, even wanting, to service masculine desire. Dworkin's *Life and Death* describes this process thus:

[In pornography, w]omen's lives are made two-dimensional and dead. We are flattened on the page or on the screen. Our vaginal lips are painted purple for the consumer to clue him in as to where to focus his attention such as it is. Our rectums are highlighted so he knows where to push. Our mouths are used and our throats are used for deep penetration. (1997:126)

The processes of depicting pornographic subjects as sexually available, subordinate, and desirous of the sexual intrusion of the consumer, it will be shown, has significant and telling ramifications for an understanding of the position of Asian men in gay male pornography.

GAY SOCIETY AND GAY MALE PORNOGRAPHY

Seemingly, pornography is an omnipresent feature of gay society in the late twentieth and early twenty-first centuries.

The production and proliferation of gay male porn, gaining its momentum from the 1969 Stonewall riots, is just one of the many paths the gay liberation movement took. If, in the early 1970s, the production, owning and viewing of pornography was a "right" of straight men, it was now also a "right" of gay men. More importantly, however, the appropriation by gay men of pornographic media was a big step toward legitimating and making visible their sexual practices. Most social movements appropriate and recodify the languages of the existing dominant social order they wish to change. Therefore, if gay men were (and still are) constructed on the basis of sex and sexuality, they must necessarily take those constructions by and for the "other" and remake them on their own terms. (Burger, 1995:3-4)

Thus, from the mythic defining moment of gay liberation and the creation of gay consciousness, the Stonewall riots, pornography has been present as an integral part of gay male life and culture. Claims that gay pornography acts to legitimate gay male sexual practices and to sexually educate gay men have, it seems, exempted gay male pornography from many of the criticisms of heterosexual pornography raised by the radical feminist movement's antipornographic analyses.

Yet, as many feminist theorists have pointed out, "[a]s men gays receive the same socialization as do heterosexual men. Dominance and submission are eroticized for them too" (Jeffreys, 1990:145). This of course carries through into gay male pornography, and especially into the pornographic materials that form the basis of this study: those featuring Asian men.

Given the negative images and stereotypes portrayed in gay male pornography, it is hard to imagine a coherent defense being mounted regarding pornography's relevance and importance within gay society at large and to the development of gay Asian society and culture in particular. Yet this is precisely what is happening.

One of the most sophisticated champions of the gay pornographic industry is John R. Burger. His *One-Handed Histories: The Eroto-Politics of Gay Male Video Pornography* (1995) mounts an articulate defense of the gay male pornographic industry. Gay male pornography, Burger argues, operates as a form of "popular memory" in the articulation, promotion, and validation of gay male identity.

> Under the aegis of popular memory, it [gay male pornography] works in a twofold manner: first as an object of study it can be read by both gays and nongays alike, as a cultural document. Second, as a dimension of political practice, it abets the reshaping, reformulation, and rethinking of gay male culture and its role in society. In short, pornography makes gay men visible. (Burger, 1995:4)

Interestingly, even one of the harshest critics of depictions of Asian men in gay male pornography, Richard Fung (1996), subscribes to this notion. Fung states:

> I think that pornography is an especially important site of struggle precisely for those Asians who are . . . economically and socially at a disadvantage, or those who are most isolated, whether in families or in rural areas; print pornography is often the first introduction to gay sexuality—before, for example, the gay and lesbian press or gay Asian support groups. But this porn provides mixed messages: it affirms gay identity articulated almost exclusively as white. Whether we like it or not, mainstream gay porn is more available to most gay Asian men than any independent work . . . That is why pornography is a subject of such concern for me. (Fung, 1996:196)

Fung's attitude seems to be one of resigned acceptance of the existence and social strength of the institution of pornography. Indeed, Fung has attempted in his outreach work to Asian gays to utilize and subvert pornographic images in the articulation of more positive images of Asian gay men (Muñoz, 1995). This is very similar in nature to the arguments of feminist libertarian proponents of pornography who promote the fact that "women should learn from porn about their sexuality. They see it as brave, exciting and rebellious to use pornography" (Jeffreys, 1990:268). Fung's position, in advocating the "cleaning up" (to adopt Sheila Jeffrey's phrase) of the most obviously problematic instances of enforced Asian submissiveness in pornography, seems to ignore the radical feminist assertion that pornography has, as its core motivation, the stimulation of those portions of the gay male erotic imagination which have been socialized to respond erotically to manifestations of supposed personal dominance over the submissive Other (Jeffreys, 1990). Fung, and others persuaded by his approach, may do well to consider the fact that the libertarian approach to pornography from within the feminist movement was spearheaded by those who championed sexual practices based around axes of dominance and submission, masked under the seemingly neutral promotion of a celebration of "desire" (Jeffreys, 1990:263). Gay men are already one of the most marginalized and despised groups within Western society, and the experience of "double disadvantage" by those who are both gay and members of an ethnic minority group, such as gay Asian men, should lead to a wariness toward any further attempts at valorizing and eroticizing (purported) characteristics of submissiveness and vulnerability.

RACIALIZING DESIRE: DEPICTIONS OF ASIAN MEN IN GAY MALE PORNOGRAPHY

It is within this domain of widespread availability and consumption of pornographic material in contemporary gay society that the circulation of gay male pornographic material featuring Asian men takes place. The process of eroticizing the exotic Other has been traced back to both colonial times and to the slave trade (see Hyam, 1986) and also has significant antecedents in the approach of the metropole to the sexual freedoms perceived to be available in the Near and Middle East (see Said, 1979). Rana Kabbani has written of the West's "insistent claim that the East was a place of lascivious sensuality" (Kabbani, 1994:6), while Edward Said has described the sexual conquest of Oriental women as representing "the pattern of relative strength between East and West and the discourse about the Orient that it enabled" (1979:6). Said presents Orientalism as a mechanism through which "the Orient is penetrated, silenced and possessed" (p. 207; see also Stoler, 1991). Yet these forms of analysis are not merely applicable to historical materials, or to the domain of colonial heterosexuality. Grant Parsons (1997) has argued that the nineteenth century colonial empires were seen as providing sanctuary and sexual prospects for European homosexual men alienated by their own cultures and societies. These characterizations have been carried forward within much of contemporary Western gay male culture, which continues to read and present Asia as a place of sexual permissiveness and opportunity. A clear example of this can be read from the text accompanying a photographic spread in a 1995 issue of the soft-pornographic magazine *OG: Oriental Guys*. Designed to complement a series of soft-core pornographic photographs of Asian men, the text clearly reinforces a homoerotically coded reading of the physical space of Asia.

> A pictorial journey into the world of sensual South East Asian men is an experience you will thoroughly enjoy and capture for yourself the colorful and exciting spirit of ASEAN in a nutshell! [sic] These guys are no muscle men nor weeny wimps but ordinary, everyday people you'll run into by the bustling sidewalks of Kuala Lumpur or the colorful bayfront by Roxas Boulevard in Manila. They are real people with genuine charm and natural courtesy waiting to meet you and become your friend in a world without strangers. (ASEAN men gallery, 1995:46)

This idyllic characterization of archipelago South East Asia as a gay paradise, complete with its unquestioned promotion of the availability and ease of interaction (and, more crudely, homosex) with Asian men is typical of the manner in which Asia is constructed within the discourse of the homoerotic imaginary (see Altman, 1995). The Western man is reassured, in this fantastic scenario, of his unquestioned attractiveness to Asian men, and the ready availability of sexual favors, due solely to a racially derived superiority over these constructed subjects of his desire. Here, the exotic, different, Othered nature of Asian men constructs Asia as diametrically opposed to the West (Foong Ling Kong, 1995). This process of "worlding" or ascribing a trope of passivity and homoeroticism to the space of Asia, when approached from a postcolonial perspective, can be read as indicating a global cartography of power aimed at perpetuating the subjugation of the Other, the non-Western, or, in this case, the Asian.

This is nowhere clearer than in the language employed by Western gay men to describe same-sex attraction to Asian gay men. David Henry Hwang's (1998) afterword to his *M. Butterfly* contains the following passage:

> Gay friends have told me of a derogatory term used in their community: "Rice Queen"—a gay Caucasian man primarily attracted to Asians. In these relationships, the Asian virtually always plays the role of the "woman"; the Rice Queen, culturally and sexually, is the "man." This pattern of relationships had become so codified that, until, recently, it was considered unnatural for gay Asians to date one another. (1998:98)

Interactions between Western gay men and Asian homosexuals— whether these be social or sexual, short-term or long—are, within Western gay male culture, often consigned to a stereotypically mapped series of clichés which characterize Asian men as passive, feminine, subordinate, and representative of the exoticness and mystery of the Asian Orient (Tsang, 1996:153). Eric Estuar Reyes (1996) writes that Asian-American gays and lesbians "are still combating representational hyphenization and stereotypes as a model minority with exotic (a)sexualities" (1996:86), while the black feminist theorist bell hooks states:

> The commodification of Otherness has been so successful because it is offered as a new delight, more intense, more satisfying than normal ways of doing and feeling. Within commodity culture, ethnicity becomes spice, seasoning that can liven up the dull dish that is mainstream white culture. (1992:23)

In the commercial realm of gay pornographic representation, Asian men become the spice of which hooks speaks, linking gay erotic imagination and the perceived submissiveness of Asian men. As Alice Y. Hom and Ming-Yuen S. Ma (1993) state:

Our (presumed) racial characteristics are fetishized by the non-API [Asian and Pacific Islander] gay communities as a frozen form of desirability—one that is derived from an Orientalist perspective. In this economy of desire, the trade is almost always unidirectional, where APIs are encouraged to use our "exotic appeal," our "Oriental sensuousness," to maximise our attractiveness to other-non-Asian and usually white-men. (1993:38)

The applicability of feminist analyses here becomes immediately apparent. The processes being described by Hom and Ma are almost identical to those identified by Dworkin when she speaks of women's bodies being fetishized in pornography (1997:127). Indeed, Dworkin talks of the sexualizing and fetishizing of the racial attributes of black women in pornography (p. 128). Parallels can be drawn between the objectification of women as passive, available, and nonthreatening through the constructions attributed to them by pornography and the processes that occur to Asian men. In 1979, following the National Third World Lesbian and Gay Conference, Michiyo Cornell decried the process of ascribing such characteristics to Asian-American lesbians and gays, stating, "We [Asian Americans] are called the model minority, the quiet passive, exotic, erotics with the slanted cunt to match our slanted eyes or the small dick to match our small size. But we are not" (1996:83).

Representations of Asian men in gay male pornography are loaded with such images of submission and dominance. For example, the pornographic magazine *OG: Oriental Guys* which caters to so-called rice queens frequently shows images of Asian men in positions of submission or servility. Issue 19, for instance, features a twenty-page photo spread titled "Hitchhiker Kidnapped!" (Stanley, 1997) and provides a pertinent example of the types of imagery which, I would argue, reinforce racially coded images of Asian submission to Western desire. The photo spread, and the accompanying text, introduces the consumer to Gary, purportedly a member of some military organization, indicated by his camouflage shorts and bandana. He is initially presented beside a road, attempting to thumb a ride from passersby. He is bare chested, with a well-defined physique, and appears to be in his early or midtwenties. As the pages of images unfold, Gary is blindfolded, bound, and thrust into a car by an unknown and unseen assailant. Indeed, in all the images that follow, one is never shown the person who is performing actions upon Gary's body, the intention presumably being to invite the spectator/consumer to imagine himself in the position of dominator. As the fantasy continues, Gary is collared, leashed, and led to some undisclosed (but nonetheless exotic and Oriental) jungle location where he is undressed, handcuffed, and bound into various poses of submission. His clothing is gradually removed, revealing his erect penis. His face, when shown, reveals changes in expression from pain and surprise in the first few photographs, to pleading and submission in the middle photographs, finally ending in an expression of ecstasy. As this change occurs, Gary is seen variously thrust into a large earthenware pot, with a leather belt draped across his bound body, and finally trussed firmly with rope and with nipple clamps attached to his erect nipples. It is by this stage that Gary is seen to be exulting in his degradation and forced submission. The final two photos show close-ups of Gary's penis forced into an elaborate cock ring and bound with metal rings, and of his anus and bound testicles. The text accompanying this fantastic scenario of domination and enforced sexual servitude rearticulates the erotic stimuli of sexualized submission with phrases (supposedly from Gary's viewpoint) such as "[t]he pain and the agony and some hidden pleasures in between. Always a potent combo" and "[h]e found himself wanting it, wanting more. More pain meant more joy sometimes. He could hardly restrain himself."

This piece of pornography has been described in such detail as it more clearly than most illuminates some of the pressing issues confronting Asian men in their attempts to reverse many of the negative stereotypes and images regarding them that are reinforced by the pornography industry. Ironically, each issue of *Oriental Guys* has, as a byline on the front cover, the words "presenting a positive image of Asian men"! But such an example should not be taken to be in any way uncommon. Richard Fung (1996), in his groundbreaking, and much anthologized, essay "Looking for My Penis: The Eroticized Asian in Gay Video Porn" demonstrates many examples of how, in bell hooks's words "race and ethnicity become commodified as resources for pleasure" (1992:23). He speaks of this in the context of gay male video pornography, with special reference to a particular Vietnamese-American pornographic "star," Sum Yung Mahn. In the cutthroat world of pornographic stardom, a porn actor's *nom de théâtre* plays an important part in identifying his sexual practices, and enticing the prospective viewer or purchaser to consume the pornographic product. Thus, names such as Randy Storm, Dick Masters, Michael Cummings, and Black Steel (names all drawn from Champions Video of Australia catalog) commonly adorn the covers of pornographic videos. Sum Yung Mahn's stage name, however, is a "trite racist pun" (Burger, 1995:56) being an "Asianized" corruption of the English phrase "some young man," further objectifying and commodifying the person of the Asian porn star in the service of Western gay male fantasies. Sum Yung Mahn's videos almost invariably have him playing a subservient role and assuming a passive sexual position. Fung analyzes three videos, wherein Sum Yung Mahn is variously presented as a stand-in for a white man in passive anal intercourse, as a sexually subservient houseboy, and as an exotic fantasy for white gay male desire. As Fung states:

> . . . the only place for a real Asian actor is as a caricature of passivity. Sum Yung Mahn does not portray an Asian, but rather the liberalization of a metaphor, so that by being passive Robbie [the white actor whose place Sum Yung Mahn takes in passive anal sex] actually becomes "Oriental." (1996:184)

Playing the passive role in anal intercourse, as constructed in gay male pornography, is most frequently portrayed as submissive behavior. Richard Dyer (1985) identifies problems with this, stating that the narratives of gay male pornography are "never organized around the desire to be fucked, but around the desire to ejaculate (whether or not following from anal intercourse)" (1985:28). Fung problematizes this with regard to the impact of racial politics in the narrative structures of pornography featuring Asian men: "the problem is not the representation of anal pleasure, per se, but rather that the narratives privilege the penis while always assigning the Asian the role of bottom; Asian and anus are conflated" (Fung, 1996:187).

This of course has immediate parallels in feminist antipornographic theorizing. As Andrea Dworkin (1988) has often pointed out, one of the objects of pornography is to conflate its subject with sexual organs or genitalia. Thus, as Dworkin states, "pornography shows women as body parts, as genitals, as vaginal slits, as nipples, as buttocks, as lips, as open wounds, as pieces" (1988:204). This occurs with Asian men in gay male pornography, who, as Fung states, are conflated with anus, with buttocks, with passivity, and with vulnerability. Nowhere is this more obvious than in the letters page of *Oriental Guys,* where Caucasian readers compliment the magazine on models or photo spreads that they have found particularly arousing. One such letter and its reply from the *OG* editorial staff will demonstrate the point at hand:

> I have recently received four back issues of *OG* and you are to be congratulated for the high quality of the editorial, design and editorial content. Would it be possible to include more "pink" that is explicit butthole pictures in each issue? Perhaps I am not alone in thinking the rosebud part of Asian men's anatomies is choice.
>
> *Reply:* No Peter you are not alone and we have already taken steps to rectify the situation. (Letter to the editor, 1995.5)

Feminist theorizing has long pointed to the influence that pornography has on socializing behavior patterns within its consumers. As Sheila Jeffreys (1990) points out, pornography "educates the male public. It would be very surprising if it did not" (p. 257). Jeffreys maintains that pornography is one of the many causal factors of the abuse of women, with consumers of the pornography acting out and realizing the fantastic pornographic scenarios with dire consequences for those whom pornography has construed as desiring and even wanting such abuse (1990:255-257). Similarly, within gay culture, the positioning of Asians as inferior, through (among other means) pornography, does have important implications for gay men. As Fung (1996) explains:

> The "ghetto," the mainstream gay movement can be a place of freedom and sexual identity. But it is also a site of racial, cultural and sexual alienation, sometimes more pronounced than in straight society. For me, sex is a source of pleasure, but also a site of humiliation and pain. Released from the social constraints against expressing overt racism in public, the intimacy of sex can provide my (non-Asian) partner an opening for letting me know my place . . . Most gay Asian men I know have similar experiences. (1996:190-191)

Fung also expands on the influence that pornographic images of Asian men engaged in homosex with Caucasians have on gay Asian men's own conceptions of their own sexuality. He states that

> [a]lthough other people's rejection (or fetishization) of us according to the established racial hierarchies may be experienced as oppressive, we are not necessarily moved to scrutinize our own desire and its relationship to the hegemonic image of the white man. (1996:184)

Hom and Ma (1993) elaborate on this theme, saying:

> Since many of us "came out" in the Euro/American gay context, our ideals of male beauty are necessarily influenced by the dominant cultural standards of beauty and desirability . . . Not only do we not see other API [Asian and Pacific Islander] men as desirable; they are almost always perceived as competition because those who are like us undermine our exoticism and our "specialness" in the eyes of the (desirable) white man. (1993: 37-38)

In an interview with Marcus O'Donnell (1997), the prominent Australian gay actor Anthony Wong also spoken against this practice, saying:

> The . . . thing I hope is changing . . . is this emasculation of Asian men—this whole portrayal of Asian men as less than masculine, as effeminate, as not as male and healthily masculine as Anglo or European men. And Asian men often perform that role thinking that this will make them more desirable and unfortunately a lot of those Anglo men who go out specifically to pick up an Asian guy that is what they want to see . . . I remember hearing an Asian guy saying "I couldn't stand having sex with another Asian man—it would be like having sex with myself." And I remember thinking, "What's wrong with that?" (O'Donnell, 1997:27)

The constructed self-hatred inherent in the denial of the attractiveness of other Asian men is obvious. This, in no small measure, may be attributed to the pervasiveness of images of Caucasian male beauty as the norm in gay society. This can be linked to the negative images of Asian men presented in both in gay male pornography and media, the privileging of Western standards of beauty and the characterization of Western men as dominant over (presumed) Asian submissiveness.

Given the construction through racially marked pornography of Asian men as invariably sexually submissive to white Western desire, the appearance within Western gay porn of alternative expressions of Asian masculinity and sexual expression might, on face value, be regarded as a small step forward. In 1997 and 1998, Catalina Video (a U.S.-based pornographic video production company) produced a number of videos featuring an actor of Asian ethnicity performing under the name Brandon Lee (the actor's stage name presumably references that of Brandon Lee, the son of kung-fu movie star Bruce Lee). What was significant about these films (which included the titles *Asian Persuasion*, *Asian Persuasion II*, *Fortune Nookie*, *Throat Spankers*, and *Dial S for Sex*) was that Lee was exclusively depicted performing the insertive sexual role in anal intercourse—both with other actors of Asian ethnicity and, significantly, with white actors. As Claudine Ko (1999) relates: "Brandon blows the notion of the submissive Asian out of the water. He never takes it in the ass . . . He's a top through and through" (Ko, 1999). But is this the major step forward it appears? Does the ability for Western pornography to depict a sexually active Asian man indicate a weakening of the racist stereotypes already discussed? A reading of some of Brandon Lee's videos, and their consumption, suggests otherwise. By far the majority of his scenes present Lee engaged in sexual encounters with other Asian men, or, where white men are present, engaged in predominantly oral intercourse. In one scene, in *Dial S for Sex*, Lee is seen providing an erotic telephone fantasy to a white actor who masturbates to climax.

Significantly, being the insertive partner in sexual intercourse is usually linked to the role that Brandon Lee is assigned to play in the pornographic fantasies. Thus, while acting as a real estate agent in *Asian Persuasion*, he anally penetrates an Asian client to clinch an apartment sale, and later goes on to anally penetrate another Asian actor who plays that staple role of the pornographic repertoire, the pool cleaner. Similarly, in *Fortune Nookie* Lee is presented as the owner/ operator of a brothel of Asian male prostitutes, one of whom provides sexual services to "the boss." Even between Asian men, within the pornographic realm, anal sex remains firmly tied to age-old structures of dominance and control, such as socioeconomic difference and the relationship between prostitute and pimp. Unsurprisingly, this eroticized inequality carries through into those instances where Brandon Lee is depicted engaging in anal sex with white actors. The opening scene of *Fortune Nookie* is a case in point. The scene opens with Lee shown inheriting his late uncle's male brothel but unable to pay the legal fees associated with his uncle's will. Consequently, a sexual bargain is struck between Lee and the Caucasian lawyer (played by porn actor Jacob Scott) whereby Lee will sexually service Scott in return for a waiver of the fees. Scott becomes the stand-in for both the movie director and the viewer's fantasy, directing Lee's character to first provide a striptease entertainment and then engage in oral sex, analingus, and finally anal sex. In the words of one pornography reviewer, Scott "controls the scene, even though Lee is the one doing the plowing" (Spencer, 1998). Throughout, Lee is shown as responding to Scott's verbal instructions, which are peppered with infantilizing and demeaning comments such as "Are you gonna fuck me like a boy or are you gonna fuck me like a man?" and "Are you man enough?" Clearly, despite Brandon Lee being the insertive partner, it is the white actor who controls the scene for his own pleasure, who is in a position to judge and control Asian masculinity—and with whom the viewer is invited to identify.

Brandon Lee has become arguably the most popular Asian pornographic actor within contemporary gay male culture and his videos have inspired a number of Internet-based fan Web sites where viewers discuss his work. These sites demonstrate just how little has changed with respect to the eroticization and racialization of dominance and submission in contemporary gay male culture. At one of the most popular Brandon Lee fan sites, hosted by Yahoo! Groups, viewers are invited to "write and share your Brandon fanfic [fan fiction], revealing all your Brandon fantasies, what you'd like to do to him, or what you'd like him to do to you—the nastier and more humiliating the better!" (BrandonLee_Gay, 2003).

Predictably, perhaps, the response to this invitation has seen the online posting of a series of sadomasochistic stories in which Lee is variously drugged, blackmailed, bound, or whipped and invariably forced to play the sexually receptive role in anal intercourse with white men. The misogynist and racist overtones to the titles of these stories, such as "Brandon Lee: Bottom Bitch" and "Asiatic Agony," scarcely require comment. What is significant, I would argue, is that Lee's expression of sexual behavior and desire not concordant with the racialized dictates of contemporary Western gay society has attracted such a strong response—and from those who claim to be Lee's strongest fans. I am reminded of an example of how such representations have been carried into the erotic consciousness of Caucasian gays, from Eric C. Wat (1996) of the Asian American Studies Center at the University of California, Los Angeles. Wat relates the story of a friend who had to convince a drunken Caucasian man that he was not prepared to play a sexually submissive role. In response to this the white man became incensed and said, "You have completely turned Americanized. Go back to Asia and learn how to be Asian" (1996:73). As Wat states: "This white man and others like him, sober or inebriated, have no way of relating to my Asian brothers except from atop" (p. 73).

CONCLUSION

Critically reading gay pornography can help illuminate the power inequalities at play within gay society and within the genre of gay porn itself. Feminist theory posits that gay men, as indeed all men, are socialized to eroticize dominance and submission. Clearly, the contents of Asian-themed gay male pornography both cater to and reinforce this eroticization. Tom Waugh (1985) has suggested that "gay porn functions as a potential regressive force, valorizing sexism, looks-ism, sizeism, racism, ageism, and so on, as well as violent behaviors" (p. 33). By branding Asian gay men with the stigmata of supposed submissiveness, exoticism, and sexual availability, Asian-themed gay pornography is complicit in propagating negative and damaging racial stereotypes.

Interestingly, radical feminism, a discourse criticized for its dismissal of issues of race, can play a large part in exploring and explaining the racism of much of Western gay porn. As Catharine MacKinnon (1989) asserted: "Inequality is what is sexualized through pornography, it is what is sexual about it. The more unequal, the more sexual" (p. 143).

Both radical feminism and postcolonialism are critically concerned with challenging structures that perpetuate and legitimate inequality. Building from this, I would hope that the forms of analysis undertaken in this chapter suggest that much can be gained from allying radical feminist perspectives with other forms of knowledge. Sheila Jeffreys pointed to these possibilities in 1990 when she concluded that "[d]ifferences of race and class can provide power differences to eroticise . . . [and that those] committed to the creation of an egalitarian sexuality must be prepared to challenge this" (1990:315). As long as desire remains ordered along racially hierarchical lines within contemporary gay society, such egalitarian sexualities become impossible to contemplate. Jackson (2000) argues persuasively that "[t]he racialisation of desire infects not only social relations and sexual and romantic relationships within gay cultures" (p. 185). If we are to arrive at a cure for this infection, pornography may have to become not just a site, but a target, of our struggle.

REFERENCES

Alcoff, Linda. (1991-1992). The problem of speaking for others. *Cultural Critique* 20:5-32.

Allyn, Eric (Ed.). (1992) *The dove coos: Nók Käo Kän'—Gay experiences by the men of Thailand.* Bangkok: Bua Luang.

Altman, Dennis (1995). The new world of "Gay Asia." In Suvendrini Perera (Ed.), *Asian and Pacific inscriptions: Identities, ethnicities, nationalities* (pp. 121-138). Bundoora, Australia: Meridian.

ASEAN men gallery. (1995). *OG: Oriental Guys* 16:46.

Bhabha, Homi K. (1994). *The location of culture.* London: Routledge.

BrandonLee_Gay. (2003). Brandon Lee—Fans of the Gay Adult Star. Yahoo! Groups. Available at http://groups.yahoo.com/group/BrandonLee_Gay/.

Burger, John R. (1995). *One-handed histories: The eroto-politics of gay male video pornography.* Binghamton, NY: Haworth Press.

Cornell, Michiyo. (1996). Living in Asian America: An Asian American lesbian's address before the Washington Monument. In Russell Leong (Ed.), *Asian American sexualities: Dimensions of the gay and lesbian experience* (pp. 83-84). London: Routledge.

Darby, Phillip. (1997). Introduction. In Phillip Darby (Ed.), *At the edge of international relations: Postcolonialism, gender and dependency* (pp. 1-10). New York: Pinter.

Darby, Phillip, Devika Goonewardene, Edgar Ng, and Simon Obendorf. (2003). A postcolonial international relations? Institute of Postcolonial Studies Occasional Papers 3, North Melbourne, Victoria.

Dworkin, Andrea. (1988). Why pornography matters to feminists. In Andrea Dworkin (Ed.) *Letters from a war zone: Writings, 1976-1987* (pp. 203-205). London: Secker & Warburg.

Dworkin, Andrea. (1997). *Life and death*. New York: Free Press.

Dworkin, Andrea and Catharine A. MacKinnon. (1988) Model antipornography civil rights ordinance. In Catharine A. MacKinnon and Andrea Dworkin (Eds.), *Pornography and civil rights: A new day for women's equality* (pp. 138-139). Minneapolis, MN: Organizing Against Pornography.

Dyer, Richard. (1985) Coming to terms: Male gay porn. *Jump Cut* 30:27-29.

Foong Ling Kong. (1995). Postcards from a yellow lady. In Suvendrini Perera (Ed.), *Asian and Pacific inscriptions: Identities, ethnicities, nationalities* (pp. 83-98). Bundoora, Australia: Meridian.

Fung, Richard. (1996). Looking for my penis: The eroticized Asian in gay video porn. In Russell Leong (Ed.), *Asian American sexualities: Dimensions of the gay and lesbian experience* (pp. 181-200). London: Routledge.

Gandhi, Leela. (1998) *Postcolonial theory: A critical introduction*. St. Leonards, Australia: Allen and Unwin.

Hom, Alice Y. and Ming-Yuen S. Ma. (1993). Premature gestures: A speculative dialogue on Asian Pacific Islander lesbian and gay writing. *Journal of Homosexuality* 26(2/3):21-51.

hooks, bell. (1992). Eating the Other. In bell hooks (Ed.), *Black looks: Race and representation* (pp. 21-39). Boston: South End Press.

Hwang, David Henry. (1998). *M. Butterfly*. New York: Plume Books.

Hyam, Ronald. (1986) Empire and sexual opportunity. *Journal of Imperial and Commonwealth History* 14(2):34-89.

Hymowitz, Kay S. (2003). Why Feminism is AWOL on Islam. *City Journal* 13(1). Available at http://www.city-journal.org/html/13_1_why_feminism.html, accessed August 30, 2003.

Jackson, Peter A. (2000). That's what rice queens study! White gay desire and representing Asian homosexualities. *Journal of Australian Studies* 65:181-189.

Jeffreys, Sheila. (1990). *Anticlimax: A feminist perspective on the sexual revolution*. New York: New York University Press.

Jonathan, David (Ed.). (1994). *The dove coos II: Gay experiences by the men of Thailand*. Bangkok: Bua Luang.

Kabbani, Rana. (1994). *Imperial fictions: Europe's myths of Orient* (2nd ed). London: Pandora.

Ko, Claudine. (1999). My search for Brandon Lee. *Giant Robot* 14. Available at http://www.giantrobot.com/issues/issue14/brandon/index.html, accessed August 30, 2003.

Letter to the editor. (1995). *OG: Oriental Guys* 14:5.

MacKinnon, Catharine A. (1989). *Toward a feminist theory of the state*. Cambridge, MA: Harvard University Press.

Muñoz, José. (1995). The autoethnographic performance: Reading Richard Fung's queer hybridity. *Screen* 36(2):84-96.

O'Donnell, Marcus. (1997). Taking no prisoners: Interview with Anthony Wong. *Outrage* 165:24-27.

Parsons, Grant. (1997). Another India: Imagining escape from the masculine self. In Phillip Darby (Ed.), *At the edge of international relations: Postcolonialism, gender and dependency* (pp.166-196). New York: Pinter.

Reyes, Eric Estuar. (1996). Strategies for queer Asian and Pacific Islander spaces. In Russell Leong (Ed.), *Asian American sexualities: Dimensions of the gay and lesbian experience* (pp. 85-90). London: Routledge.

Rudy, Kathy. (2001). Radical feminism, lesbian separatism and queer theory. *Feminist Studies* 27(1):191-222.

Said, Edward W. (1979). *Orientalism.* New York: Vintage Books.

Spencer, Jeremy. (1998). Review: *Fortune nookie. Behind closed doors* 51(December 17). Available at http://www.gayvideodad.com, accessed August 30, 2003.

Stanley, George (photographer). (1997). Hitchhiker kidnapped! *OG: Oriental Guys* 19:53-72.

Stoler, Ann Laura. (1991). Carnal knowledge and imperial power: Gender, race and morality in colonial Asia. In Michaela di Leonardo (Ed.), *Gender at the crossroads of knowledge: Feminist anthropology in the postmodern era* (pp. 51-101). Berkeley: University of California Press.

Stoller, Robert J. (1972). Pornography and perversion. In David Holbrook (Ed.), *The case against pornography* (pp. 111-128). London: Tom Stacy Ltd.

Tong, Rosemarie Putnam. (1998). *Feminist thought: A more comprehensive introduction.* Boulder, CO: Westview Press.

Tsang, Daniel C. (1996). Notes on queer "N" Asian virtual sex. In Russell Leong (Ed.), *Asian American sexualities: Dimensions of the gay and lesbian experience* (pp. 153-162). London: Routledge.

Wat, Eric C. (1996). Preserving the paradox: Stories from a gay-loh. In Russell Leong (Ed.), *Asian American sexualities: Dimensions of the gay and lesbian experience* (pp. 71-82). London: Routledge.

Waugh, Tom. (1985). Men's pornography: Gay vs straight. *Jump Cut* 30:30-35.

Index

Order a copy of this book with this form or online at:

http://www.haworthpress.com/store/product.asp?sku=5437

GENDERED OUTCASTS AND SEXUAL OUTLAWS
Sexual Oppression and Gender Hierarchies in Queer Men's Lives

_____in hardbound at $29.95 (ISBN-13: 978-1-56023-500-2; ISBN-10: 1-56023-500-4)

_____in softbound at $16.95 (ISBN-13: 978-1-56023-501-9; ISBN-10: 1-56023-501-2)

Or order online and use special offer code HEC25 in the shopping cart.

COST OF BOOKS_____

☐ **BILL ME LATER:** (Bill-me option is good on US/Canada/Mexico orders only; not good to jobbers, wholesalers, or subscription agencies.)

☐ Check here if billing address is different from shipping address and attach purchase order and billing address information.

POSTAGE & HANDLING_____
(US: $4.00 for first book & $1.50 for each additional book)
(Outside US: $5.00 for first book & $2.00 for each additional book)

Signature_____

SUBTOTAL_____

☐ **PAYMENT ENCLOSED: $_____**

IN CANADA: ADD 7% GST_____

☐ **PLEASE CHARGE TO MY CREDIT CARD.**

STATE TAX_____
(NJ, NY, OH, MN, CA, IL, IN, PA, & SD residents, add appropriate local sales tax)

☐ Visa ☐ MasterCard ☐ AmEx ☐ Discover
☐ Diner's Club ☐ Eurocard ☐ JCB

Account # _____

FINAL TOTAL_____
(If paying in Canadian funds, convert using the current exchange rate, UNESCO coupons welcome)

Exp. Date_____

Signature_____

Prices in US dollars and subject to change without notice.

NAME_____

INSTITUTION_____

ADDRESS_____

CITY_____

STATE/ZIP_____

COUNTRY_____ COUNTY (NY residents only)_____

TEL_____ FAX_____

E-MAIL_____

May we use your e-mail address for confirmations and other types of information? ☐ Yes ☐ No
We appreciate receiving your e-mail address and fax number. Haworth would like to e-mail or fax special discount offers to you, as a preferred customer. **We will never share, rent, or exchange your e-mail address or fax number.** We regard such actions as an invasion of your privacy.

Order From Your Local Bookstore or Directly From

The Haworth Press, Inc.

10 Alice Street, Binghamton, New York 13904-1580 • USA
TELEPHONE: 1-800-HAWORTH (1-800-429-6784) / Outside US/Canada: (607) 722-5857
FAX: 1-800-895-0582 / Outside US/Canada: (607) 771-0012
E-mail to: orders@haworthpress.com

For orders outside US and Canada, you may wish to order through your local sales representative, distributor, or bookseller.
For information, see http://haworthpress.com/distributors

(Discounts are available for individual orders in US and Canada only, not booksellers/distributors.)

PLEASE PHOTOCOPY THIS FORM FOR YOUR PERSONAL USE.

http://www.HaworthPress.com

BOF06